TALES OF BODY AND SOUL

TALES OF BODY AND SOUL

LIONEL BLUE

Hodder & Stoughton
LONDON SYDNEY AUCKLAND

First published in 1994
by Hodder & Stoughton

10 9 8 7 6 5 4 3 2 1

British Library Cataloguing in Publication Data

Blue, Lionel
Tales of Body and Soul
I. Title
828.91402

ISBN 0 7472 4335 2

Typeset by
Letterpart Limited, Reigate, Surrey

Printed and bound in Great Britain by
Mackays of Chatham PLC, Chatham, Kent

Hodder & Stoughton
A division of Hodder Headline PLC
338 Euston Road
London NW1 3BH

To those who helped me with this book —
my mother and aunt,
Celia, Peggy and Vivien
Jim, Eric and Theo

Contents

PREFACE

Each of us has a private scripture, not about how God appeared to other people at other times, but about how God appears to us now.

Some of us keep it secret to ourselves. Some of us confide it to those we love. Some, like me, publish parts of it.

Such private scriptures are made up of small incidents which, as we continue to ponder them, turn into modest parables. Don't discard your own parables; they are your life experience. In them is the pattern and purpose you seek.

DO-IT-YOURSELF RELIGION

Role-Playing

For twenty happy years, I ran the religious court of the Reform synagogues in this country. On my desk I had a little plaque which read, 'If you believe in me, I exist'. Theoretically, as Jewish canon law covers every conceivable situation – and many inconceivable ones – in this world (though not the next), the whole world was my responsibility. In practice, I dealt with conversion, religious divorce, status, adoption, tombstones and rows, for a minority of a minority. My colleagues married people florally and chorally on Sundays, and on Mondays I cleared away the debris and divorced them. Some of my colleagues thought I was marginalised, but I didn't see it like that. You don't need much religion to get married – nature does the work for you. You need much more to negotiate a decent divorce.

When I asked one of my colleagues why I had been appointed, because my antinomian cloven hoof was only half hidden, he gave a reply so sensible that my opinion of the establishment shot up. 'Because,' he said, 'you like saying yes to people.' Which is very true. It's easier to say no to people, because then *voilà*, the problem's solved – though it isn't. 'Yes' or 'maybe' mean yet another problem – oy, oy, oy and God go with you! He probably does, because He's the only reason why a sane religious bureaucrat with an instinct for self-survival invites trouble.

The trouble is that religion and reality have parted company and they'll never come back together again in the old way. The evidence is everywhere, though only my court work made me see the obvious.

When I was apprenticed to an older rabbi, I noticed that the advice he gave from his pulpit didn't tally with the advice he offered in his private office. When I remonstrated (I was a pious prig), he said, 'Lionel, in the pulpit you give general rules but regard anyone who comes to you privately as an exception.' Like many compassionate clergymen, he was nicer than his religion and I was touched, but then I had second thoughts and became wary. It was just a kinder restatement of a situation which is undermining religious credibility: when the rabbi says one thing and the congregation keep another, and the rabbi knows they keep another, and the congregation know that he knows they keep another, and he knows they know he knows . . . And on and on and on till the conspiracy of silence collapses credibility in anything. Sure, no one means any harm. They're in a fix, that's all, and playing safe, which in spiritual matters means playing very dangerous indeed.

You can call it what you like. Role-playing is the polite word. But what does role-playing mean when it's at home — acting!

A notice should be stuck on every prayer book: 'Religious role-playing can seriously damage your integrity'.

Do-It-Yourself Religion

If you censor things like sex and ambition out of life, you falsify people and they become unreal — and so does their religion, because then they don't tell God what they really think, but what they think God thinks they ought to think — which gets nobody nowhere.

Where Does God Live?

A retired missionary from China told me of a curious visit he made to an ancient Chinese shrine where, in spite of himself, he was impressed by the faith of the worshippers who venerated the holy stone walls and fixed prayer flags in them.

He asked a young monk who spoke English, 'What do you all pray for?'

'World peace and harmony,' replied the young man courteously.

'And are your prayers ever answered?'

The monk giggled. 'Sir, you might as well talk to a brick wall!'

When I am invited to a conference in a part of London I haven't set foot in for years, I decide to take a sentimental detour to get a glimpse of my old bedsit. But it's so long ago that I can't even remember the house, though I do recognise the church that I used to meditate in. But it's changed. I'm startled by its fresh paint, curtains and dolphin door-knocker.

My companion explains how the church was abandoned except by the winos, until it was cut up into 'character' flats. That accounts for the door-knocker.

There are many holy places like that now, secularised or bolted shut because the vandals have returned. 'London's losing its soul,' I complain to my friend. But he is unsympathetic. 'They couldn't have been that wonderful or they wouldn't have been left to the winos. They're more useful as they are.'

I want to argue but I remember that retired missionary who would have agreed with him. Perhaps God prefers winos. Perhaps He's still present at the same address, helping the yuppies in the smart flats to stay true to each other.

The missionary used to say, 'Faith is spirit, not buildings, and God's at home wherever we allow Him to be Himself.'

Out of the Religious Ghetto

I sat in the train to London, reading my newspaper, thinking New Year thoughts, when suddenly a wave of gratitude washed over me for some Christians I'd met. I put down my paper and took out a notepad instead, because I wanted to jot down some thank-yous. It's not so usual for a person of one faith to say nice things about another, because the big religions are competitive like businesses, but that's what God prompted me to do.

I wanted to thank some nuns for their non-Christmas party. They were worried their non-Christian friends might feel left out, so they organised one specially for them, with pressies and games and a vegetarian pud, but with no mention of Christmas. It was a very Christian thing to do and much appreciated. Thank you, Sisters!

And the mention of food reminded me of the Christian retreat houses I visited who altered their menus and programmes to fit in with non-Christian food laws and festivals.

At mealtimes they taught me that Jews have no monopoly of religious fun and I pass on to Christians this grace I heard in one of them:

'For bacon and for buttered toast,
Praise Father, Son and Holy Ghost.'

9

Of course, if you wander out of your own religious ghetto, it's not all ecumenical fun. You can't avoid some bumps and bruises. A speaker at one retreat said innocently, 'Without Christ, you can't be fully human.' So what was I, then? He just wasn't used to having other faiths around.

I also wanted to thank a Christian lady whose name I don't know, for hand-washing the soiled underwear of an AIDS patient she didn't know. But I know and God knows.

And there was a Christian man who visited the ward armed with tracts and pamphlets. But he didn't press them on a patient. 'He's worried enough already,' he whispered, 'I won't make it worse.' I was so impressed, *I* read his pamphlets instead.

After I finished my thank-yous, I picked up my newspaper again. It was depressing reading. Every nationality and community in Europe was taking umbrage and clamouring for its rights.

There were so many of them, I sighed, most of them right but in conflict with each other's rights. Fortunately, some people like my Christians don't insist on their rights, but forego them. It's called renunciation, and without it our planet will blow itself up and then rights won't matter, for none of us will be left to claim them.

Quality Religion

I sit on a platform with representatives of other faiths. The chairman poses prepared questions and awaits our familiar answers.

'In this day and age, should religion give a lead to politicians?'

'Yes,' rings out one speaker and earns a nod. I say that I'm not sure, and get a warning look.

I'm in the doghouse again. But is religion always a good thing? True, it abolished slavery, taught spiritual truths and gave the downtrodden dignity. But it also supported slavery, was downright dishonest and suppressed anyone who disagreed. So how do you separate good and bad religion, or tell which is which?

At first, I thought you could separate religions into quality ones and second-rate ones, but it's impossible to judge. Most of us only know the religion we're born into. Then I thought the traditionalists were the goodies and the modernists the baddies, and later on the other way round – but I've been both and owe my faith to both.

A clue came from the Talmud. The schools of Hillel and Shammai disagreed constantly, but the Talmud says that God preferred the Hillelites because they listened sympathetically to their opponents, even quoting their views before their own. In other words, it isn't just what you believe but the way you hold your beliefs that matters.

There's no shortage of religion in the Middle East and in what was once Yugoslavia, but only the best quality religion will do any good in either, for in politics, second-rate religion only makes bad worse.

And to the Talmud's politeness test for religious quality, I would also add the humour test, because jokes deflate pretensions. I became more optimistic after a friend of mine, an ardent Israeli nationalist, told me this story.

When God asked Moses what land he should promise him, Moses was so overcome he stammered, 'Ca – Ca – Ca –',

'Oh, you want Canaan,' interrupted God kindly. 'Well, that's nothing to write home about, so I'll promise it to you.' But what poor Moses was trying to say was California – which explains a lot! And I hope the Palestinians can respond with a similar story of their own . . .

Yes, religion *can* give a lead to politicians and leaven their lumpy anger and recriminations, provided it's the best quality religion, the courteous listening kind. And its holiness will be even more effective if it is accompanied by a little unholy laughter.

God in Our Pockets

I went into religion because I was bored and sex-starved, and because candles and cosmic voices hotted up a drab time. I enjoyed it but didn't believe in it till the first bump, when instead of me using it, my inner voice started to use me, making me give away things to other people. I decided to ditch it but found I couldn't.

At first, services turned me on, especially when I could prance about in processions. But one day the service fell as flat as a pancake and I wondered whether to stop studying for the ministry. Then to my relief, my inner voice resurfaced in more normal places like parks, bars and package holidays.

Later on, I got another jolt while preaching a safe sermon. 'Do you really believe that?' said my inner voice. I didn't know and had to do some painful self-analysis and study to find out.

But this year came the biggest bump of all – a real lulu. That inner voice which had supported me for forty years walked out on me. 'Goodbye,' it said, and was gone. That was that.

I've accepted my loss now. I think my inner voice has moved into me, that's all, and become part of me. My religion no longer needs special sound effects. It can be ordinary.

Which has had an odd side-effect. It's made me think of all the atheists and agnostics who do good without voices or visions or the consolations of religion. Ministers like me must irritate them dreadfully. We seem so certain about God and His likes and dislikes, as if we've got religion in our pockets. It isn't quite like that.

That goodness we all serve is a great mystery. For some, like me, it's personal and has a human face. For you, maybe, it's the unexpected resources of love and service inside you. We only begin to understand it as we practise it.

Thank you for keeping an open mind about my own and other people's beliefs.

Become Your Own Evidence

In Eastern Europe, you never got hot news from the newspapers but from jokes whispered among friends. "What's up? Have you heard the latest?"

A Stalinist party desperately looks for new members. If you recruit one, you'll get fifty roubles reward. For two new members, you'll get fifty roubles and permission to leave the party yourself. And if you recruit three, you'll get fifty roubles and a certificate that you were never a member of the party in the first place.

In its heyday, Stalinism worked rather like a religion. It had its sacred writings and heresies and it demanded complete commitment. No wonder some disillusioned party members now turn to religion, because it has a familiar feel. A market economy may satisfy your hungry body, but only belief can satisfy a hungry spirit.

Forty years ago, I was having my first doubts about materialism, but I didn't find the change-over to religion easy. Three problems worried me and my experience then may help others on the same path now.

The first was not what religion said but how it said it – through stories, myths and parables, not scientific statements, and if you're modern, this makes you want to give up. But Stalinism wasn't as scientific as it sounded, and Bible stories aren't as artless as they seem.

15

Next problem. Did I have to believe the lot? Forty years ago, I tried to and got religious indigestion. Take a text like, 'I once was young and am now grown old but have never seen the righteous forsaken nor his seed begging bread.' Well, the psalmist might not, but I have — many times. So I consider the statement; I don't pray it. Though I use my grandpa's prayer book, I can't be my own grandpa. Our life experience isn't the same. Yet when I pray, I link mine to his and that feels loyal and honest.

And now bull's-eye. Are these stories fairy stories, comforting opium as Marx said? What's the evidence?

I first looked for it in books and other people, but they contradicted each other or had feet of clay. Then one morning in the ugly chapel of Balliol, I realised you become your own evidence as you watch the God you worship remake you in Its image. Religious questions always boomerang back at you.

An old-time party member told me in tears that the revolution got hijacked because of personal ambition, greed and power. 'We tried to understand society to change it,' he said, 'but we didn't start with ourselves.'

And this sad statement reminds me. Have you heard the latest?

Some hard-liners pray for Stalin to return to earth.

'Come back, Comrade Stalin, and restore the party.'

'OK,' says Uncle Joe grudgingly, 'but I warn you — this time no more Mr Nice Guy.'

16

Piety and Consumerism

The lady before me at the supermarket check-out chats about recipes, and recipes lead on to religion. 'The fish and chips at Lourdes', she said, 'was bril!' Holiness always makes her hungry. My holy places, I tell her, are also connected with food, though more humdrum – like this supermarket. She's interested, but her turn's come and she can't concentrate on both piety and prices.

But it's true – ten minutes of shopping and mild consumerism quieten me as much as meditation, though I only buy an avocado. I don't know why, but it's like that with a lot of people.

And in supermarkets you get glimpses of heaven and hell, just like Dante in *The Divine Comedy*. There's the man looking so innocent, producing his credit card in the 'cash only' queue, after they've rung up his goods. There's a woman counting out a mountain of small change in the fast lane, avoiding the eyes of the harassed housewives behind her. And you sometimes notice half-empty beer cans and half-eaten chocolate bars behind the stacks.

But there's a touch of paradise too. A woman sees you're in a hurry and lets you take her turn. A mum with two kids picks up items that tumbled from your trolley. And because I look poor and scruffy, a pensioner points to a notice and tells me to wait five minutes, when they'll reduce cakes and biscuits.

I also read the notices on cans and packets

carefully because I'm on a low cholesterol diet and I marvel at the precision of their contents and claims – E this and E that, "specially suitable for diabetics, with only 41 kcal and 0.7 grams of fat". It makes me think of my own merchandise, which is of course religion, and wonder if I can be anywhere near so precise. Like many Jews of my generation, I don't want to claim too much – there were too many unanswered prayers on the way to the gas chambers for that.

OK, say you're not religious and you ask me what you can really get out of religion. What could I say from my own experience? Here goes and I'll try not to exaggerate.

It has taught me other people are as real as me and God loves them as much as me, so I mustn't manipulate them.

It's turned the pain and problems of my life into compassion and pity for myself and others, not anger.

It helps to release me from worldly success and failure.

It's put me in touch with a 'beyond life' which props me up and takes away the fear of death.

It's given me purpose.

It's taught me to trust.

Though it's illogical, I've found some sort of inner divine friend.

It sounds more than I thought. I'm really rather surprised how many goodies I can list on my religious package.

Outside the supermarkets the beggars who used

to lie in wait outside churches and synagogues have made the same connection as me. They too have made a connection between piety and consumerism.

A lady offers one of them a small bar of chocolate.

'The Belgian ones are better,' says the tramp judicially.

'And so is the price', says his indignant benefactor.

'Believe me, lady,' he says with conviction, 'it's worth the extra.'

Honesty

The children in the Sunday School asked me what is my favourite virtue. I didn't choose charity, which is warm and what they wanted, but honesty which is basic but more brutal. I was honest in telling them I'd always been too insecure to be good at it, but I was getting better. I wasn't so honest in telling them the curious ways I'd learnt it.

I learnt some of it on an analyst's couch because, being a gay man, I had to live a lie for many years and loathed it. I actually got to enjoy being open and honest in Communist East Berlin, of all places. They bugged my restaurant table, and I was warned they even bugged hotel bidets and eavesdropped on your prayers. Against such technology, I stood no chance, so I prattled away frankly to my unseen listeners on food, faith and Christian–Jewish relations.

I felt slighted when they never used my material but later on I learnt they'd overbugged, couldn't cope with all those endless snores and grunts, and were five years behind in monitoring their tapes.

Modern technology might make honesty easier for the kids too, I thought. A businessman proudly showed me his briefcase. It contained a lie-detector and a device to listen to what your neighbours were saying next door, so you could learn straight away what your best friends didn't dare tell you. How could the next generation help being honest?

One perceptive lad at Sunday School pointed out I'd never mentioned religion. He was right. To be honest, religion is better at charity than honesty – there's too much role-playing and regard for institutions. And being honest with God can be awkward – because we expect God to expect too much from us.

When I went on an oldies holiday to Portugal, I prayed in restored synagogues and meditated at shrines. But in a bar at Fatima, I had to admit in all honesty that the oomph had gone out of my prayers. My personal relationship with God had gone cold, but why?

To be honest, perhaps I no longer needed a divine father to make up for the one I'd lost, nor a divine brother to replace the one I never had, or as a stand-in for the lover I longed for. I'd grown up and heaven no longer had to make up for any family deficiencies. Was anything religious left in me, I wondered? What would life be like as a humanist?

And then in Lisbon on the last day of my holiday, it hit me and my religion was turned inside out. What I needed from God and how I used or misused Him was irrelevant and not worth worrying about – it was what He needed from me that was important. What you give to life matters much more than what you get out of it. My former religion was only a preparation for the real thing.

Honesty had forced me to solve my spiritual problem, not cover it up, and I was so pleased to get God back on any terms and so relieved not to have to change my profession that I pressed six hundred escudos on to a surprised beggar in relief.

In religion, as in a good marriage, you divorce, rediscover and remarry your partner many times.

The Best Fuel

For many people, living on the fringe of organised religion, the old mythologised extended family is a beautiful bygone, belonging more to *Fiddler on the Roof* country than to modern inner cities and suburbs, and they are the fall-out.

Now if such people were just spiritually poor or bankrupt, then we could organise a classical cure. Missionise them! Up and at 'em – though with compassion, of course. The problem is that although many of them may not be (probably are not) card-carrying religious members, they can be very spiritual indeed. Too spiritual, in fact, and way beyond the charity committees and formal liturgy of official faith. They have more faith than they realise, just as there is more doubt in the establishment than it is prepared to admit.

One characteristic of their spiritual search became obvious to me from working in the media, from retreats and hospital visiting.

What propels their spiritual search is need – the best fuel of all. If you haven't got an extended family, for example, then you have to make your own out of friends – that's the reality of life in a big city. The old home rituals, suitably adapted, though without benefit of clergy, do just that. Therefore, the rise of religious friendship groups like Jewish Chavurot (holy friendship circles) and Christian housechurches. Gays and lesbians also need spirituality because their faithfulness and commitment have to come from something inside themselves, not from institutions or external approval. So they pray a lot – not politely but practically. Many, living alone in bedsits for whatever reason, age or HIV, feel marginalised by Religion with a capital R and therefore turn to religion with a small r to turn their loneliness into solitude.

They all ask 'absurd' questions, which are sensible in their situation: 'Rabbi, where should I park my car on the Sabbath, outside the synagogue or two streets away?' 'Do lesbians need a religious divorce if they've had a religious blessing?' 'My wife keeps Easter, I keep Passover; how do we combine?'

After all, the Talmud says God didn't reveal himself to angels but to ordinary human beings. And the people who followed Jesus or who stood at the foot of Mount Sinai were also outsiders, and searchers who didn't fit in.

Making Room

Forty years ago, my religious organisation decided to revise its liturgy, and battle commenced between the oldsters who wanted to Thee-Thou the Almighty, and the youngsters who wanted to You-You Him.

The You-You-ers won, and a rabbinical student and I were entrusted with the revision. For thirty-five years, it was our companion, and our excitement too – because the prayer book is the only holy book which can still grow with the life experience of its users.

It grew with the arrival of women rabbis. A prayer which began, 'I am a man poor in good deeds,' became outdated before it was printed. And then God along with His ministers ceased to be a simple He – which wasn't surprising, as Scripture and tradition had long ago likened Him to a midwife, widow and mother hen.

The last development and the nicest has just happened as our work is coming to a close. For the Jewish harvest festival, a booth is built to re-experience the wanderings in the wilderness. In it, the worshippers eat and pray, welcoming their friends and the Jewish great and good of long ago, whose writings they read. Well, some of the non-Jewish great and good are being invited too, to acknowledge the obvious: that like the harvest, no group has a monopoly of divine goodness. So the ghosts of King Alfred and Mrs Gaskell will rub shoulders with Talmudic sages and the spirit of George Fox will chat with Jewish mystics.

Such mutual recognition has become urgent, when communal killings have stirred up hatred, and partisan religion has blackened the name of God in India, the Middle East, Bosnia and even here.

We cannot combine religions, I know. But we can make room in our own liturgies to acknowledge the holiness in each other's faiths and learn from it. It brings back to life what we already possess, but have taken for granted.

Life's a Gamble

A young couple ask me to make a speech at their wedding, just as I did for their parents. I'm touched, and can't resist telling them about the weddings of long ago, when the guests who'd drunk their fill tried to he helpful and prompt the rabbi, with uncertain results.

'In our cheneration,' proclaimed a bearded sage, 've are fighting ze bettle of, of . . .'

'Britain,' shouted the guests.

'Chewdaism,' glared back the affronted sage.

Booze wasn't a real danger, because Jews talk too much to be serious drinkers. In any case, the wine they liked at those far-off weddings was so sweet that you got sick before you got drunk.

The real problem was cards, I tell the couple. After God had been blessed and the Queen toasted, guests, groom, cantor and choristers settled down to serious pontoon, while wives with heaving bosoms urged on their weaker spouses. The tactics were basic. They simply raised the stakes to see who lost their nerve first, although as they only won and lost from each other, no one came to grief.

The couple start to look anxious, but I assure them that I wasn't bitten by the gambling bug, and only play Scrabble. They look relieved and go. And yet, looking back on it, I was bitten more than I realised and became the biggest gambler of them all, because I bet my life on God. Religion isn't the insurance people think.

Many people try to prove or disprove God with arguments, texts and miracles, but in the end the arguments cancel each other out, so like any gambler, you back your hunch. Not because of what you get out of it, because often all you get out of religion is a load of trouble. Belief is more like an addiction, a passion, a falling in love that proves itself only in your own experience.

A lot of life's a gamble. Even in the Bible, leaders are chosen by lot. And today, for example, finding the right partner still needs luck – as does keeping your health into old age. Even such a serious matter as the Jericho–Gaza breakthrough is a gamble. Please God it brings permanent peace, but like all other political breakthroughs, it could set off results no one can foresee. In the end, even canny politicians have to take a risk and make a leap of faith, just like the humblest believer, hoping God will bring good out of it.

Sometimes He does, and sometimes He doesn't seem to, and that has to be faced as well. But then, as my gambling forebears would say, a bet is no sure thing, and if you're a believer, you back God both ways: to win or to lose. Though being no gambler, I didn't understand the technicalities, those words struck home – that is why I continue with religion, because when I look back on my life, I only regret the times I didn't bet on God. I have never regretted the times when I did, even though things didn't always work out the way I wanted. As a believer, I'm content to back Him both ways, whether I 'win' or 'lose' in a worldly sense. The passing of the years has only made this faith firmer, and in fact I have even increased my bet.

The Places Nice Sermons
Don't Reach

My little court of religious law for Reform Jews was
tucked away at the end of a corridor. People came
to me to be divorced and I had to handle some of
my clients with kid gloves. They were angry with
religion and I sympathised, for they got more
sermons than support. But paradoxically, because
they had less use for religion, they had more need of
God. Social structures couldn't give them the
strength their situation needed. It had to come from
the God within them.

There were step-parents who needed it to love the
children of their divorced predecessors. Gay couples
needed it to create the commitment and fidelity
religious rituals couldn't provide. Divorced people
needed it to be content with their own company.
Modern families needed it to include within their
warmth a puzzling new mixture of relationships
and faiths.

One lady needed it badly. I was surprised to
meet her at a party, because our host was her
former husband. 'Get yourself a drink,' he sang
out from the hall. Without thinking, she relapsed
into her old hostess routine – the house and the
furniture were so familiar. She poured drinks for
everybody and was just about to press one on her
successor when she remembered where she was,

33

sat down abruptly and conscientiously played second fiddle for the rest of the evening.

'I thought you were going to faint,' I whispered.

'Not fainting, crying "Help!" ' she said laconically. 'You need an awful lot of God to get to the places nice sermons don't reach, rabbi.'

Like many clerics, I used to lament the absence of God in modern life. I think I looked for Him in the wrong place: because my studies had concentrated so much on past and future religious glories, I didn't see Him in the messy present. To my surprise, I began to see that He was very present in the tangled problems life presented to my little office.

MAKING A LIVING

When the World Goes Bust

When I was accepted as a rabbinical student, an old German rabbi was appointed to act as my tutor on practical ministerial skills. I duly called on him to discover him and his wife kneeling on the floor, painting the boards that showed through, with the pattern of their carpet, so that their congregation would not notice the holes. With dignity, they accepted my offer of help and my first tutorial took place on all fours. I learnt how to travel third-class but appear out of a first-class door on arrival, and was exhorted to invest in handmade black shoes, silk socks and engraved, not printed, visiting cards.

These requirements meant real sacrifices, as our salaries were inadequate and we had no pension arrangements. Many grave and learned colleagues survived on discreet hand-outs at weddings and funerals. But our status was assured, even if our emoluments were not. We were always served first at dinner and, representing the Almighty, we took precedence over all other professionals unless they were peers. We were proud of our position in society and once suited with a congregation, we assumed we would remain with it for ever.

Modern students for the ministry in their jeans and sneakers are amused by such past pretensions and tell me they have it easier. There are proper pension arrangements now and salaries scaled to those of senior teachers. But it seems to me they have exchanged one form of insecurity for another which is far worse, because they will be judged by results and must therefore keep on their toes. Younger colleagues, after all, come cheaper in a recession, even religion must be cost-effective. Also, like everybody else, they are subject to even more pressure than before, being urged by unceasing advertisements to want things they do not need. It is harder to teach the good life in such circumstances.

What is happening to rabbis is now happening to the entire middle class and, on balance, modern insecure affluence is more difficult to handle spiritually than the genteel poverty of the past.

I therefore pass on to you as well as my students another old-fashioned lesson from my former tutor: invest part of yourself in a world that does not change by meditating for five minutes every morning on your own Last Judgment. It may sound macabre but you will find, as the fear of God builds up in you, that it will release you from other fears, so that even if your outer world goes bust, as so many middle-class worlds have done, your inner dignity and integrity will not go bust with it.

As to his other advice, I shall occasionally out of respect conduct services in long, black silk socks. It is still possible to buy them in charity shops, but I wouldn't bother if I were you.

Self-Employed

In the bookshop, I bumped into a woman who said she recognised me on TV. Do I recognise her, she asked. There was something familiar about her and, prompted, I remembered we used to do our homework together. I was an unattractive child but she was nice about it.

'What's with you?' I asked her. She told me she was made redundant a few years ago and, rather than moulder in a dole queue, she staked her savings on a one-woman business. 'It's lonely but I get by – just,' she said. And I suddenly wanted to hug her and all like her who've taken on the recession single-handed. There are lots of plaques in churches to soldiers, sailors and civil servants, but not many to small business people, though they're the unsung heroes of our day.

I wasn't made redundant myself, but I can understand how she feels because I also resigned from my safe job a few years back to be a writer, broadcaster, retreat runner, after-dinner speaker, and cook.

'Being a celebrity, you must do pretty well,' she said without rancour.

'About the same as a teacher or lecturer,' I told her, 'but I do the work I want. Freedom and security don't come together.'

We chatted on about the self-employed state: dividing your earnings by seven forty-sevenths to work out your VAT, how nobody wants you or everybody wants you at once, and having to celebrate your successes alone.

Religion is so preoccupied with sex and theological infighting that it doesn't bother enough about small business people – which is a pity, because religion certainly gave me practical help both times I've worked for myself.

Having no fixed week, for example, I needed the Sabbath to make myself take a rest and realised God's greatest invention was the weekend.

Also, not having to clock in, I needed prayer to build me up and get me up. So as soon as I opened my eyes, I made a habit of thanking God for all the things I'd done right, and the courage and bounce he'd created in me. Then I used to shout 'Amen', leaping out of bed and landing on my dog. There was no going back to bed after that!

Does prayer work? Even for business people who have to be hard-headed? It has never moved mountains outside me, but it has removed obstacles within me, helping me to fill in forms which frighten me, or answering the phone when I'm low.

But being self-employed, you can also feel unsupported and lonely, so your spirits go up and down like a yoyo according to other people's opinions. Which is why I go to retreat houses to strengthen my own centre – to save my soul, if you like. The people who run them may not know much about business – though even hermits earn their keep these days – but they're on your side and they give you their attention for free.

Religion also has some unexpected consolations if you're just starting up. A chap asked his minister, 'Can I live a decent life on sixty pounds a week?'

'My child,' said the minister compassionately, 'it's the only life you could lead.'

The Bottom Line

Black Wednesday really affected me, because I actually dreamed the devaluation was going to happen, but didn't do a thing about it. This was partly because I didn't want to seem like a speculator, but mainly because I couldn't be bothered to find out how you deal in Deutschmarks.

Afterwards I could have kicked myself and I consulted a colleague, who'd lost more than I'll ever make and survived, to find out whether Scripture had helped him.

'When I felt suicidal,' he said, 'the best spiritual advice actually came from a solicitor who told me bluntly, "Forget the trimmings and phantasies; what's the bottom line you have to preserve, to survive?" It was my family and work. The rest was trimmings.'

At home I brooded over this. It's true! God can't be confined to any ghetto and He speaks through the honest advice of secular accountants, doctors and therapists, as well as through rituals and religious talks.

At a conference afterwards, I complimented a waitress on her efficiency. She told me she used to be a Lloyds name. But after an associate had a heart attack, she decided to become a waitress. She said she had no regrets and had never felt so fulfilled in her life.

That's the spirit,' I told her, for she practised

what John of the Cross preached, finding a light in the darkness of financial despair. For her, the bottom line was concern for others and getting a good night's sleep.

Two centuries ago, Rabbi Nachman predicted that progress would make life more precarious, not less. He compared it to crossing an abyss on a rope bridge – and not being afraid.

Success

The recession lingered on like a headache, disrupting people's lives. Some applied for enterprise grants. Some became monks, seeking security in heaven. Some considered marriage, because then at least there's someone to complain to or about. Some even consulted ministers of religion like me, though economics confuse me, and I'm terrified by tax forms.

I was amazed when a friend asked me whether or not he should set up his own business. There were so many unknown factors that he was going out of his mind, and was reduced to asking me for advice.

'I can't even begin to understand your problem, let alone solve it,' I said humbly. 'But here's a story which may take the edge off it. A great rabbi once said that there are two ways to success in archery. The first way, you practise for years, then you hang your target on a wall, and shoot at the bull's-eye with all your skill and concentration. The second way is much simpler. Don't bother to practise. Just shoot your arrow at the wall, and wherever it hits, draw your target round it.

'Think about it,' I told him. 'It's not just about archery, but about happiness. Our difficulties in life don't come from God but from ourselves.' He telephoned me a few days later and told me it had helped.

And if you too are tossing and turning, worrying

whether you'll make it, do try to relax! Life is short and the point of it isn't worldly success; it's about turning our selfishness into generosity and our aggression into kindness. God is concerned with what we are, not with what we have. Whether you make it materially or not doesn't alter the real purpose of your life on earth.

Rich and Poor

Long, long ago, during the last recession but one, I told the joke about the Liverpool chap who harangues a crowd on a pier.

'Don't save me,' he says. 'I've had enough.' And he throws off his coat and his shoes and plop! He's in the Mersey.

Immediately, a second man throws off his coat and shoes and dives in after him. As he swims up, the first man cries, 'Don't save me. I've had enough.'

'I'm not trying to save you, mate,' came the reply. 'I just want to know where you work.'

As the recession grew worse, so my old joke acquired a newer, grimmer sequel. When the second man applies for the first man's job, they tell him it's already taken – by the man who pushed him in!

I offer some spiritual tips to help you save your own soul, if not your savings, in times of recession. None of them is original. They come from my listeners. I only pass them on.

A cabby who'd been a chauffeur quoted Larry Adler to me. The great harmonica player, he said, had felt bitterness as a kid because he had no shoes. Until, that is, he met a man who had no legs! Remember Britain's still one of the richest countries of the world and we're jolly lucky to live in it. If you personally want to feel rich, then give something to someone poorer than you – there are lots around.

An unemployed girl said, 'Even though your holiday money's been devalued, make sure your friendships aren't.' I agree. So ring up someone you know who's had it rough. That's real religion. Perhaps you can't give much, but you can listen.

In a crowded cafe, I shared a table with a silent woman and her abusive son, who flounced off in a huff.

'No work for two years,' she confided. 'That's why he's got such a short fuse.'

She was right. There's so much frustration around, so stand outside your own and keep quiet about it if you can. God will notice, even if nobody else does.

What Are You Worth?

Having fits is a funny business. First you feel muzzy, then lights flash, then colours drain away and life's like the picture on an old black and white TV set. Then the pavement meets you fast, without being properly introduced. Now where was I? Ah yes, then you wake up in a hospital cubicle and concerned people in pinnies furiously embroider your scalp like a practice run for the Bayeux Tapestry. Then they're rushed off to the next human repair job, but kindly leave you a cup of tea which you sip as you try to remember what really happened.

There have been other occasions, but this time I was laughing at masks of politicians with funny noses in a novelty shop window when I went down, so my fit wasn't just funny peculiar, it was also funny ha-ha – which annoys me. If only I'd been doing something more distinguished like browsing through rare books, or selecting fine wines. Well, that's something my little problem has taught me – I never knew I was such a snob.

On reflection, I realised blacking out wasn't my problem. As I was unconscious, it was a non-event. What upset me was not being able to work afterwards, because without work I feel worthless. But then I thought of all the people, unwaged, unemployed or whatever, who'd given me so much in the last year. Two AIDS chaps cheering each other up as they were going blind. A mentally handicapped

49

child who redefined success and failure. My unemployed friends, whose self-respect came from within. Some nuns who left tomorrow to God, and my old mother and aunt who could turn a hospital visit into a treat.

A businessman in the midst of the recession sighed, 'When you don't know what your house is worth, and whether your business is worth anything at all, you have to find your own worth inside yourself.' It is when we go looking for it in the wrong places that we fail to find it.

GIVING AS AN ART

Givers and Takers

My old rabbi once said, 'Judaism is your religious home, Lionel; it's not your religious prison.' This gave me courage, when my own tradition had gone stale on me, to take spiritual Awaydays, to see God afresh.

And that's how for several years I came to call on a Hindu swami before breakfast. He used to ask me what had happened to me on the way.

'I passed a beggar and gave him half a crown,' I said, overwhelmed by my own virtue.

'Why so much?' asked the swami with a twinkle in his eye.

'To help him, of course,' I answered virtuously.

'And did it?'

'Well, no, he'll buy booze. I did it to help God – it's what my grandmother taught me.'

'And does God need your half-crown?'

'He can't,' I answered sulkily. 'It's His already. I gave it to the beggar to help me, to make me feel good.'

'A very proper and religious answer,' approved the swami. Relationships are never what they seem. The taker also gives and the giver always takes.

It's a disconcerting truth I experienced once again, after my mother and my aunt moved to a retirement home.

To my surprise, they've adapted beautifully. My mother looks years younger as she touches her toes in 'Music and Movement', and my aunt is learning new tricks like singing 'Nessun Dorma' while brushing her false teeth. They're having a ball.

But for those of us who've looked after them for ten years, the pluses and minuses are more complicated. Yes, the social worker said we did well, and there's certainly more house room, and my mother no longer disturbs me, fretting whether she's taken her own tablets or my aunt's. But the old ladies gave things you can't calculate.

You see, their weakness gave us all a common purpose, which forged neighbours, friends and even strangers into a family. A Chinese waiter brought back a five-pound note my mother had left him as a tip, and their old boot repairer only wanted two smiles and a joke, not payment. For the first time, I saw an ordinary London suburban street through God's eyes and behold, it was good – for we were all givers and takers, just as my swami said.

And the same applies to my relationship with God. My prayer life has gone flat once again, so I've decided to drop the 'parent in the sky' part, with me asking for things like a child, and Him giving them – perhaps! Instead, some role-reversal is called for, and I think He wants it too. I'll be the giver for a while and He can be the taker. He'll become for me that beggar, elderly people like my mother and my aunt, a Lloyds loser I know, and the HIV people I meet on retreat. I give them my time and my money. They give me back my religion.

Karl Marx said, 'You have nothing to lose but

your chains.' But think carefully before you throw away your chains of commitment and duty, lest you lose the very things that make your life worthwhile.

Compassion

If you're a professionally helpful person, such as a social worker, therapist or minister like me, you sometimes learn what life's like at the receiving end of welfare. If you have an accident, or have to go into hospital, as I did when I had an epileptic fit, you know you're a prospective patient too and you don't get so uppish.

Disability also reveals a lot about your fellow human beings. Some are superstitious and don't want to come too close because you're bad luck and they don't want to catch it. Never mind; lepers, skin-cancer sufferers and AIDS victims all get a bigger brush-off than epileptics, and this stops me feeling sorry for myself.

Also there's much more original goodness in ordinary people than I ever credited, after they've overcome their fear. As I lay in Casualty, I remembered one lady who left a five-pound note pinned to my lapel together with a tract – which was very generous, as she must have thought I was drunk or gaga. And an antique dealer brought out a Chippendale chair for me to convulse on, which was most gracious. A pity my colleagues never saw me on it!

I try not to blame people who don't want to know. For one thing, there's too much recrimination around already. Also they're more sick than me though they don't realise it. And, after all, I've never seen myself in action, so to speak, and it must look more grisly than it is.

If disability worries you, there's a traditional blessing which might help you to cope when you see someone you think is grotesque or deformed, or who hasn't been wired up right like me: 'Blessed art Thou, O Lord our God, who varies the forms of Thy creatures.'

Varies – that's a wise, tactful word which puts it all in perspective.

Charity

The Hebrew month of Cheshvan always falls in November. My Sunday School teacher used to call it Marcheshvan or Bitter Cheshvan, because it was the only Hebrew month without a festival.

Which is why I was allowed to conduct my first public services then, though only for unimportant congregations in hired halls.

Only a handful of worshippers struggled through the autumn rain to join me. The chairman set out the chairs while I plugged in the eternal light. The ladies produced flasks of hot coffee and as the harmonium wheezed, we wheezed, sneezed and coughed along with it. Sometimes a tramp peered in, curious about the cacophony inside. He got coffee too and, when the service ended, was taken aback by a hug as we giggled, 'Good Sabbaths', surprised at what had got into us.

I was duly promoted to better things, taking crowded festival services for established congregations. Just as I was about to start one service, a warden whispered that a drunk wanted to join us. No, he wasn't exactly difficult, but he might be a nuisance with the mayor there. 'I'll keep him in your office,' he suggested. It sounded sensible, so I nodded and signalled for the choir to start up.

The service went well; I shook hands with the mayor and feeling pleased, decided to give my drunk five bob. But he refused that and our food, and politely left. And I've never got him out of my mind. My common sense tells me, don't be silly, but my uncommon sense says, perhaps God visited me in disguise but it was inconvenient and I shooed Him away.

What would you have done in my place?

At Christmas

Forty years ago, when I was a young minister, I always gave a sermon in the run-up to Chanukah and Christmas, denouncing commercialism.

But now I'm older and more honest, I have to admit there's a lot of commercialism I like. I like the glitter of tinsel, and window-shopping in London's West End. I prefer some TV adverts to the programmes they interrupt, and some of the objects they advertise make me a nicer human being. Since I got my dishwasher, for example, I no longer hate my guests when they leave me with their dirty plates. Dishwashers and word processors are fine; I'd just like there to be more of them for everybody. The material world isn't wicked, just limited, but not dangerous if you respect its limitations.

It's no use, for example, giving lavish presents to buy love – because love can't be bought. It's also no use giving lavish presents to hide your own lack of love. You don't fool anybody, even yourself.

Whatever gift catalogues say, presents needn't be commercial. The best festival present you can give your family is permission to be themselves. Adults at parties behave like children in playgrounds. One is always moody and another won't play. Respecting their feelings is a real kindness.

And the best present you can give yourself also isn't a thing but time. Book a half day in your diary – not to be the happy hostess or dutiful child, but you. And don't let anyone whittle it away.

Also you have to do something for God, otherwise you feel a fraud. That means giving of yourself, not just your money. My aunt's home help suggested visiting an old or disabled person, because during the holidays the social services run down. But don't expect rapture in return. Many old and disabled people loathe public festivals which make them feel more out of it than ever. And that is very good for your soul – because then you've done something for God without a worldly reward.

When there's so much outward religion around, be careful too not to smother God under too many packets and bottles, and even rituals, because they can hide Him too, though that's not the intention.

If your family gets difficult and your plans don't work out, don't get upset. Perhaps it's the only way God can get through to you, to tell you something important. And remember the spirit bloweth where it listeth and God is very unexpected. You might want to meet Him looking your pious best, lighting candles. But He might prefer to come and comfort you while you're washing up and weepy, because then you're not putting on the religious style and, though it's hard to believe, He loves you as you are.

Giving Without Strings

For twelve years, I shared a house with my old mother and aunt. It worked well, because a friend acted as a buffer. He came down for breakfast one day and discovered my mother dressing behind the dining-room door.

'Lionel told you to dress in your bedroom,' he said gently.

'I'll remember that,' said my mother – which she won't because she's ninety and can't.

In the kitchen, he stumbled over her sister, who's lost her false teeth.

'Hetty's half-dressed in the dining room,' he tells her.

'What? What?' mumbled my aunt, who's hard of hearing.

'Hetty's in the dining room,' he bellowed, 'half-dressed!' My aunt continued searching in the waste bin for her dentures and remarked, 'Hmm, some people would pay money to see that!'

My friend and I fell about with laughter – living with the old ladies was a delight. But eventually I took them to a retirement home for a trial week. Because although the home care was wonderful, they would soon need more.

They looked the home over. It was bright and uncrowded, for the Jewish community, like some others, is kind to its old folk. But for my aunt it had one great drawback: it had too many old people.

'So you want to retire to a youth hostel?' I asked jokingly.

'Yes,' she answered simply, 'I would!' And we all fell silent.

But my mother chirped in, 'Lil, we'll be OK. You can tell your jokes, and I'll do the typing and we'll chat everybody up.' My aunt looked at my mother wryly, for her shower hat was askew and she would not be staff, but resident.

Even so, I think my mother's less muddled about the big things than me. But then she was brought up before the hedonistic society that followed the war, and wasn't caught up as we were, in the search for happiness.

We certainly tried. The sexual binge of the Sixties was followed by flower-power, yogie-bogie and cosmic bliss through LSD. After that, there was get-rich-quick, therapy on the cheap, sects, cults, *la dolce vita*, charismatic arm-waving and now self-empowerment. Most of them were much too self-indulgent to work.

Now my mother's trying to say that happiness is only a by-product of thinking about others more, and yourself less – which is old hat and banal but true. In homes, hospitals and hospices, the discontented ones are the selfish ones, and the happy ones are the givers. And since the world's got more takers than givers, the latter are never redundant.

A social worker asked me if my mother's religious. Well, she's a believer but not pious, and calls clergy crows because of their black gear. But a conventional black crow once defined religion for me as the art of giving without strings. So, yes, she is, and her religion which served her well in our old house will serve her well in her new home, and in whatever eternal home awaits her after that.

Real Listening

He's been a good friend and I decide to do something special for his birthday. I hesitate over a continental weekend, which isn't cheap, but I anticipate his astonished pleasure and book it.

He is astonished but not pleased. He prefers home comforts, he tells me, to lugging my cases about, and has said so many times. I feel hurt. He says I never listen, like most Jews, and we sulk in silence, munching birthday cake.

The scenario feels so familiar and I wonder uneasily if he's right. Perhaps I don't listen. My family certainly never listened to me when they skimped to turn me into a solicitor, despite my childhood protests. 'We know what you want to be,' they said. 'You only *think* you do!' Which floored me. And when I became a rabbi in revenge, I was taught to preach but not to listen.

So on my first hospital visits, I used to burst in, babbling, 'Good morning! You do look well. My, what a nice ward!' While the patients watched me in silence, knowing I wouldn't listen to their despair because I couldn't – I was too scared.

You can cover up not listening more craftily by repeating catchphrases like, 'I hear what you're saying', which usually means you don't.

You can play the same tricks on God too, praying so fervently that He can't get a word in edgeways, which is a pious way of killing prayer. Or you can tell Him what you think He ought to tell you – like a charismatic couple who came to dinner. She was worried by some domestic problem. 'Pray to God,' he urged her, 'and when He tells you to take my advice, I'll be right behind you.'

It's also tempting not to listen to painful, heartrending news and tune in instead to wall-to-wall Mozart – till the suffering's been replaced by something cosier.

The reason we don't want to listen is that fear I felt in the hospital – that God or the problems of other people might make demands on us we can't fulfil, so we panic and close our ears.

If you're tempted to close your ears, this text from the Talmud might help: 'It's not your obligation to complete the work but you are not permitted to refrain from it either', which means real listening does require your response and you've got to do something about it that's within your possibilities. But don't try for impossibilities, because then you'll give up and won't listen to any cry for help. You'll just retreat to Mozart.

So what's possible, for example, after listening to the day's news?

Well, you can't stop the conflict around the world or remove military regimes single-handed, but you can certainly give something to a charity. You can try to make sure you're not a little dictator with an outsize ego, too. And you can overcome your prejudices and pray for your enemies.

THE DARK SIDE

Prejudice

I'm still haunted by the jokes I heard in my childhood, from the Jewish refugees who were trying to
escape from hell to anywhere that would let them
in. There weren't many places that would, so even
the slums of London's East End seemed like paradise.

This was one of them. A woman battles for days
at the doors of a consulate, begging for visas for her
children, her parents, herself. The exhausted clerk
says, 'Visas? That's a laugh. Come back in ten
years' time.' 'A.m. or p.m.?' asks the desperate
woman. OK, it's not very funny, but you get the
flavour.

Some non-Jewish friends say I'm paranoid and
obsessed about anti-Semitism – like most Jews.
Perhaps they're right. There are Jewish jokes about
that too. A Jew who's had one too many walks into
a wall. 'Anti-Semite,' he shouts at it.

Perhaps I am paranoid but I can't forget a card on
my desk which says, 'Just because you're paranoid,
it doesn't mean they're not out to get you.' That's a
Jewish experience, too.

Some months ago I came back from the Continent really shaken, wondering for the first time
since the forties if my old fears were again becoming
fact. Racism had returned to Europe in a big way.
Prejudice had learnt the tricks of fashion. It had
acquired a yuppie look and wore designer clothes.

Nationalism was 'in' again. But it didn't necessarily mean you loved your own land and people more. Just that you liked the others less. People made catty remarks about foreigners and thought they were clever. God help us, I thought, perhaps the Nazi horrors weren't a freak one-off. Perhaps they are a foretaste of things to come.

So how do we stop dragging each other down into hell as we did before? I suppose, being rational people, we've got to learn to like each other and iron out the little differences that divide us. But life isn't as simple as that. Those little differences of food, custom, noise level and dress can drive us round the bend. Some of my non-Jewish friends say in exasperation, 'Why do you Jews always answer one question with another?' To which the Jewish answer is, 'Why not?' which makes them more annoyed than ever. Also the people you are trying to like may not be likeable – nor may you, for that matter.

Which brings me to the religious point: if you can't like them, you'll have to love them instead. And you can start by praying for them today. It sounds more difficult, but it isn't, because when you bring God into a situation, the results will surprise you – provided you keep at it. As any alcoholic can tell you, things really happen when you invoke a power greater than yourself.

Courage

When we lack the courage to face the unpleasant-ness inside ourselves, that is how a Bosnia can happen.

On the news one day, a lady wept over the paradise that Bosnia once had been. Muslims, Jews, Croats and Serbs used to live alongside each other, and their children played together. Now those children were murdering their former playmates. 'How could it happen?' she cried.

I'll tell her how, and you too, not from textbooks but from experience.

There's hidden rage in all of us and if you can't admit it, you say it's in others and then hate them for the things you can't abide in yourself.

The Nazis did it to the Jews, the Bosnians are doing it to each other, and every day people turn their families and businesses into little Bosnias, because they're running away from themselves.

The peace process in Bosnia can only succeed if all the aggressors admit they are murderers, as well as victims. This takes real courage. But God gives it to every one of us, if we're brave enough to see ourselves as we really are – nastiness, neurosis, warts and all.

Facing Your Fears

I used to lie awake in the mornings, so scared of the world that I couldn't even get out of bed.

Well, the panic hasn't completely disappeared, but I've learnt to understand it, and even to joke about it. And when I faced up to it, help came from many sources – human, animal and divine. Therapy taught me to understand it, and my big black dog, whose four paws stood for food, food, sex and food, forced me out of bed to buy her dog-chocs, wearing a raincoat over my pyjamas. Then prayer showed me how to use my fears to understand others, turning it into a blessing.

Some weeks back, when I was weakened by flu, the old panic returned.

I had to give a lecture to a society and I knew I ought to phone them because I wasn't up to it. But I couldn't. My silly panic convinced me that *They* wouldn't believe me. I anticipated their incredulous 'Oh, I see,' and cringed.

My self-pity then turned into anger. How dare they doubt me when my throat was on fire?

While brooding on the supposed injustice, the doorbell rang. I tottered down and opened the door to two fundamentalists distributing tracts. 'Don't badger me, I'm ill,' I said and shut the door on them.

'How can they be so nasty to me?' I asked God piteously.

'Are they nasty to you, or are you nasty to them?' He answered gently.

He was right because later the society sent me a cake, and the fundamentalists only wanted to do my shopping. My fear had turned them into bad guys.

I wasn't really frightened of what others wanted to do to me, but of what I wanted to do to them. Be less frightened of others, and more of yourself.

Casting Out Demons

I want to tell you about a lecture that I went to recently that greatly disturbed me. 'From a loo in heaven above,' said the lecturer, 'a giant turd dropped down, scoring a direct hit on a cathedral below.'

'Hmm,' I thought, 'Providence has at last shown what it thinks of us humans.'

'Now before you bombard me with complaints signed "Disgusted of Dagenham", let me assure you it was only a dream – a most significant and meaningful dream,' said the lecturer, 'of the great psychologist and religious thinker, Carl Gustav Jung.' A famous dream, too, though I'd never heard of it, having fallen among Freudians.

I missed his next few remarks, because I was too absorbed by the audience's reactions. Most coped calmly; some tried to look semi-detached, and some looked round brightly as if such defecatory flying objects were only too common in their experience. But though I listened with only half an ear, I did gather that the dream was trying to warn Jung, and all of us too, not to separate our religion from our shadow side, our sense of the divine from the demons that inhabit the recesses of our minds. The dream certainly startled me, though it didn't shock me. But an earnest, gentle young minister was deeply shaken, and I had to comfort him over coffee.

He had conscientiously tried to explore his rejected shadow side, uncovered the usual demons, and they'd given him a fright.

Among other horrors, he recognised for the first time in himself the normal human aggressions, his racist and sexist thoughts when he stood in a queue, his impulse to strangle some of his congregants and his fantasy that his colleagues were all conspiring against him. 'How do I cast out my demons?' he groaned in agitation.

Since the demons of aggression are part of our human inheritance, I pass on to you two of the tips I offered him. First, ask God for courage to get acquainted with your demons. Regard your mind as a cinema screen and examine your phantasies as they flicker across it. Secondly, don't be too afraid of them, for they are only shadows which inhabit your mind and not the real world, and sensible people usually have enough common sense not to translate their fantasies into fact. Which is why, thank God, people like Hitler are fortunately few.

'But if they're only shadows,' protested the young minister eagerly, 'why can't I let sleeping demons lie?'

I'd have liked to let him off the hook but I remembered the poppy I pin in my lapel for Remembrance Sunday and thought of the dead on the Somme, the pogroms of Kristallnacht over fifty years ago, and the atrocities of Bosnia.

'Because you might think only nasty wicked people persecute others or commit atrocities, not nice people like us – which is a comforting but very dangerous illusion, and would mean that the dead of two world wars suffered and died in vain.'

It's uncomfortable bringing our demons into the light of the divine, but unless we do, they might come into their own again, and we could be the next victims, or even worse – the next aggressors.

The Fruity Curse

Some of you asked me after I received hate mail at Christmas how I got rid of my own hate – because in a time of racism and recession there's a lot of it around, and prayer doesn't always seem to shift it.

Here's an East European Jewish suggestion. Curse it away! But make your curses so fruity that your hate evaporates and you fall about with laughter. It's such an effective spiritual therapy.

You can use these examples as models:

'May your house have a hundred rooms, each with a hundred beds and may you have bad nights on all of them.'

'May all your teeth fall out except one, so that you may still get toothache.'

And more subtly: 'May your son, Mrs Cohen, meet a fine upstanding Jewish doctor.'

Madness

I was buttonholed by a chap rummaging through remaindered books, which surprised me, for he dislikes religion and rabbis. After assuring me glee-fully my own books would end up there, he couldn't contain himself about a find that a friend of his had tracked down – a Nazi pamphlet advising troops on active service to avoid unauthorised prostitutes because of the risk of syphilis. Since the only diagnosis for that disease had been discovered by a Jew, troops should prefer continence until the arrival of an Aryan cure.

'I must get it for my weirdo section,' he said determinedly, 'to add to my books on the yellow peril, the Protocols of the Elders of Zion, proposals to plough up post-war Germany, how a European nation was founded by the fairies and the holocaust never happened.

'It'll be a big collection,' he added thoughtfully, 'because Europe's going bonkers again. The hooli-gans, terrorists and nationalist bang-bangs are just the first symptoms. And this time, it'll be easier to slip madness into people's minds. Hitler only had the radio. The new lot can play with subliminal TV.'

'Perhaps religion can help,' I added timidly, and headed off an explosion by hastily gabbling a black, political joke, to which he is partial.

An English tourist in a Bavarian beer hall can't believe his eyes when he sees a Hitler look-alike at the next table. Unable to help himself, he leans over and says, 'Do you know, you look just like Adolf Hitler!'

The man regards him coldly. 'I *am* Adolf Hitler,' he answers curtly. 'Don't believe all that nonsense about my dying in the ruins of Berlin – naturally I arranged my escape.'

'But what do you do now?' asked the amazed tourist.

'I plan the Fourth Reich, of course.'

'And what will you do in it?'

'Kill another six million Jews and seven postmen,' said Hitler with a gleam in his eye.

'But why seven postmen?'

Hitler looked at him smugly. 'You prove my theory,' he said. 'Everyone will be so worked up about the seven postmen, who will notice six million Jews!'

My acquaintance decides it's funny, and I hastily say goodbye before he blows up again. But I don't think it is just funny, because the Hitler madness hasn't ended – indeed, it may be a prelude to worse things to come.

And in the new Europe which is being born amid wrangling and recession, religion remains more indispensable than ever, despite its compromises and weaknesses. The 'Internationale' failed to unite the human race as it claimed, but the words of the prophet, 'Hath not one father created us?' might just succeed where it failed.

For sane religion can help us not to make devils out of people we disagree with, whatever their class, race or sex – for that's the way back to madness and murder.

Why not do yourself, God and other people a favour today and personally reduce the level of madness in the world? Try being objective about the people you don't like, the woman who slips her car in front of yours, for example, or the chap who gets the job you needed. It's not easy, is it?

Through analysis and therapy, I've learnt the hard way to spot the irrationality, the madness if you like, in myself and others – but to control it and use it creatively, I have to call on God.

The Refugees and the Sequence Dancers

I only got down to my post last week, because I went up north to cook Christmas dinner for a friend. But the letters from my listeners were worth waiting for because they were so affectionate. One had a poem, and another a drawing, and someone said it with smoked trout. One chap sent me jokes – not quite right, he said, for Radio 4.

Well, I needed them all when I opened a glossy card with no name and a false address. It festered with hate. The sender derided the holocaust, yet regretted that one too few had been gassed in it – perhaps me or another recipient, and then jeered at poor Ann Frank, the Dutch girl who kept a diary in hiding, and who died in the camps. It was very, very nasty.

I froze, and then my lips moved in prayer. I prayed, 'When you who sent this card die and come to your Last Judgment, may the tears of the children lined up before the gas chambers and the old people herded into cattle trucks weigh in God's balance against you.' It was not a nice prayer but it was a just one, because for me death is not the end, and we all carry the consequences of our deeds across it.

Later on in a silent chapel, I meditated on hate – a sickness of the soul that is infectious and can be caught by nations and religions as well as individuals. Some, like Ann Frank, are immune from hate, and we call them saints – but I am not, nor are most of you. In fact, I had just caught a bit of it from the sender.

You can catch hate early in childhood from some real or imagined injustice, or later on if your security or self-esteem are mortally wounded – by becoming unemployed or destitute, for example. Which is why I think that without spiritual hygiene, it could become an epidemic in the nineties.

Hate, of course, never solves the problem that causes it. People usually hate in others the hateful things they can't face in themselves. Unlike anger, it's irrational.

'The refugees are responsible for all Europe's problems,' shouted the neo-Nazi.

'The refugees and the sequence dancers,' whispered the refugee.

'Why the sequence dancers?'

'Why the poor refugees?'

The silence in the chapel was very powerful. It forced me to recognise the sender as another wounded, dangerous human being trapped in his or her own hate. The memory of Ann Frank helped me to pray with all my heart for his repentance and that some compassion would steal into his heart – and mine too. For I believe that hate is only love turned sour, that has gone back on itself, and if you have the courage to make one small move out of it, the groundswell of God – His angels, if you like – come to help you.

Exorcising Ghosts

When the Jewish High Holy Days begin, I take down my prayer book to prepare myself. The liturgy excites me, as it does every year, with its promise that old things can pass away and never more be remembered. But it's never worked with me like that, and, no longer having a congregation, I can now afford to say so. The alms-giving and fasting and prayers can't flush my bad memories out of my system.

I used to think I might be able to help others if not myself – but perhaps I was fooling myself there too. I should have remembered what happened when I first started taking High Holy Day services nearly forty years ago.

A granny told me in tears that my service had changed the life of her grandson.

'Thank God, not me,' I said unctuously.

But next week, in a fight with his former girlfriend and her admirer, he gave her admirer a sock in the kisser and, not unnaturally, she intervened and bit him back. Sermons don't last long.

I put down my prayer book and try to work out what goes wrong. Why does the magic never work for me? Is it me or the book? And what can remove the burden of bad memories?

Therapy certainly helped me to put the memories in perspective. And I also remember a shrine in Malta which had a letter-box in which you posted your problems. I still wonder where my letters ended up and who read them.

A lot of things went wrong when I was there – not least the finish of a long friendship, the longest I've ever had. As a result, comfort eating made me enormous. And though I liked the people and even tried to learn their language, the place became a bad memory for me and I hadn't been back for nearly twenty years.

Perhaps I needed to. Perhaps the only way to rid oneself of bad memories is to face them head on. Perhaps it was wrong to ask God to remove them. I should pray for courage instead to exorcise my own ghosts.

I suddenly knew why those services had never worked for me. Rituals and sermons are not religion themselves, just the recipe for it. To make the religion real, you have to translate them into your life. I'd been expecting magic, not religion. Making things disappear is magic, but religion means the opposite: facing old memories, learning to live with them, and using them for good. So instead of covering them in ritual, I will pluck up courage and book a cheap package to Malta.

In Europe we're creating bad memories fast – it's our growth industry. Villages in Bosnia, hostels in Rostock are becoming accursed places. Religion is once again too weak to stop the horrors of selfish nationalism, and low-grade religion even helps it. This must be faced. But perhaps in twenty years' time, its rituals will give another generation courage to face the past without excuses, and cast out the demons that lurk there. That's my hope, before the curse becomes permanent.

A Cargo of Anger

Last week, I meditated in an empty synagogue. Instead of the usual friendly feelings, I was startled and shaken by a wave of anger, my own, which welled up inside me that I couldn't control. All the little grudges I thought I'd forgotten, inflated in my mind. I was obsessed by what I'd been done out of and by people who'd done the dirty on me. It was like watching a late-night horror show; I couldn't switch off.

I tried to think of God instead, but I suddenly knew God didn't want me to use Him as a refuge. 'Have courage,' He seemed to say – so I prayed for courage to face my own anger. The main cause of it was my own weakness. Many times when I should have spoken up, I didn't because it wasn't politic or popular, and so the unspoken truth had festered inside me.

But it's not right to carry a cargo of suppressed anger around with you. Not just because it can personally cause you migraines and depressions, but because it can also affect other people, and politics too. A demagogue can add together our little angers and grouches, turn them into one big grouch and harness it for his own purposes, and that's how Hitlers come to power.

PRAYER IN PRACTICE

The Tuesday Help

On Tuesday mornings, when I give my *Pause For Thought*, I also give a thought to my listeners. Some of them may be poorly in bed, of course, but most of them will be up by a quarter past nine and I imagine them stuck in some traffic jam, swearing blue murder, or gazing sulkily at the sink, hoping the grease will get rid of itself like it does in adverts.

My own Tuesday morning problem isn't driving, because I'm not allowed to, nor washing up, because I've bought a dishwasher. My problem is veins and arteries – my own, yours or anybody's. The sight of them makes me feel faint, which is why I became a minister, not a doctor.

But I still have to visit a lady I know with varicose veins, and help an AIDS sufferer find a fresh juicy vein for yet another injection, and the only thing which helps me not to pass out is the shortest prayer I know – 'Help!' It works because I get just enough to forget my hang-ups and the nausea only returns when I'm no longer with them but alone with time to think about myself instead.

Prayer doesn't work miracles for me. It only gives me that extra strength to do what I've got to do.

But don't take my word, even for that. Just cry, 'Help Lord!' yourself, if you get stuck one morning and see what happens.

Holding God's Hand

I wake up at night and turn on my transistor to fill the room with noise because, like many people, I tell myself I want peace and quietness, but underneath, I can't cope with silence – it frightens me. Don't be ashamed of admitting it!

Silence frightens lots of other clerics, too. Many mystics can't stop talking. I remember some rabbis came together to organise a retreat on silence. There'd be a talk on 'Silence in Jewish Tradition', to please the traditionalists, and another on 'Silence as Psychotherapy' for the modernists. The keynote speech would be on 'Silence in Liturgy'. It all came together beautifully, till my secretary pointed out diffidently there wasn't a single minute's silence left in the entire programme.

Congregations deceive themselves about silence. They say they want it, but two minutes' tight-lipped nothingness is as much as they can take. So first, they introduce an organ for background muzak, and then with a meditation to begin and a prayer to end, the silence is squeezed out of the sandwich. Perhaps nothing will happen, in which case, where is God? Or even more disturbing, something will speak in the silence and God is only too present. Which is the more frightening?

If you do find yourself in a silent house or hotel

at night, don't fight it. Sit up in a comfortable chair and savour it. Sip the silence, so to speak, and make friends with it, because it's got a lot to tell you.

This is what happens to me. First, leftovers of worry float through my mind. Did I turn the gas off, and did I leave a ten-pound note in my trousers? I let that fluff settle, but more lies underneath.

I remember all my sillinesses, some of them sexual, and I squirm, wondering how I could have let them all happen. The embarrassment then turns into pain, and all the bitterness and rejection I suffered floods into my mind.

I'm awash with anger, shocked by the strength of my own feelings. They drain me and tears come. I sit back exhausted, wishing I'd kept to safe prayers and left silence alone.

In the distance, I hear the honking of distant traffic, and people's chatter through an open window. They seem friendly, and I feel close to them. I look around my room, and notice the delicate interplay of light and shade. Somehow everything seems right just as it is. And then, very deep within me, a surge of gratitude wells up and flushes away my anxiety and mess. I feel washed out but clean.

And I feel moved to pray – not necessarily in words. Sometimes it's only a melody out of tune, faint, but the beginning of joy is in it.

And when the tune dies away, I sit quietly, blessing myself with the silence. I feel as if I am holding God's hand.

I've found out what's at the centre of the silence. But in religion, never take things on trust. To get to that centre never takes me less than ten minutes – but it doesn't take me more than twenty either. Tomorrow night, give it a try.

Prayers Answered

Some people say that because God hears prayers, He'll give you what you ask for and that will make you happy. I agree that He hears prayers, but He can answer those prayers in such a backhanded way, I recommend caution.

Consider this case of a Jewish lad who rings up his mother to tell her he's in love.

'Her name's Mary Magdalene O'Murphy,' he sighs.

'How can you mention such a name to your Yiddishe momme?' she sobs, and hangs up.

Some months later he calls her from America. 'I'm in love again,' he sighs.

'What's her name?' asks his mother suspiciously.

'Miss Goldberg,' he replies.

'Goldberg, a fine Jewish name,' cries his mother. 'God has answered my prayers.'

'That's nice, mum,' he replies, 'and her first name's Whoopi.'

Be a Radio

About fifty years ago, my family emerged from an air-raid shelter to see if our house was still standing. Well, it wasn't – there was just a smoking black hole. The wardens could hear noises, and thought someone was buried alive but it was only our old Bakelite radio, still playing 'Run, Rabbit, Run' with its bottom blown off, which was a giggle – the only one that morning. Once again I was grateful to the BBC.

I had a lot to be grateful for. The Beeb had altered my accent, softening my cockney Yiddish twang, though I still say 'thinkink' when I'm excited – not 'thinking'. *Children's Hour* also changed my class, introducing me to a dream world of nannies and nurseries, where unemployment was unknown.

That gratitude still remains, and I enjoy going to Broadcasting House an hour before I need on Monday mornings for *Thought For the Day*. There are lots of perks. I cadge concert tickets from the foyer desk, read the agony aunts in the tabloids and sometimes, in the classier corridors, salvage from the leftover trays bits of smoked salmon undented by human teeth, either false or true.

But I'm not just a materialist on the make. I also arrive early to improve myself and to translate the Latin inscription above the lifts. '*In hoc templum artium et musarum*' . . . In this temple of the arts and muses . . . but just a minute, shouldn't the neuter be *hocum*? It's nearly a half century since I parsed Latin verbs and declined nouns – so perhaps it's the other way round.

In that foyer, I also realise that I myself am a human radio that can tune in to God, and when I do, it subtly alters my script.

For example, it takes my mind off that script and makes me think of the listeners instead. Often the difference between a piety and platitude isn't the words you say but the warmth in them. A consummate actor could counterfeit this feeling – but I'm not, thank God, and can't. And also when I've written something clever but unkind, which is easy, tuning in makes me realise it's only clever-clever and so I cut it out, which is more difficult.

This fine-tuning on to God's wavelength takes time and trouble. His voice is a still, small one; coming from such a strange dimension, it's a wonder we can catch it at all. Also it's difficult separating it from the crackle and static of our neuroses and egos.

These tips may help. If the voice you get sounds grandiose or grabby, and makes you high, you're on the wrong station. The real voice is unobtrusive. It sounds like kind common sense.

It usually takes me ten minutes to locate the wavelength, which is why I arrive early. But try it yourself, because you're a radio receiver too, and probably a later model than me.

HOLIDAYS AND THE HAPPINESS PROBLEM

Sun, Sea and Spirit

During my ordination examination, my Talmud teacher suddenly unbent like a benevolent crocodile. My mouth dropped open in astonishment like a terrified fish as his umlaut-laden voice whispered in my ear that I had a wonderful future ahead of me in Aramaic verbs. Perhaps he was going deaf. Perhaps I'd just struck lucky, but no one has since repeated this remarkable prophecy, or bothered about my verbs either.

I have been bothered instead by matters which my teacher would have despised, such as happiness and holidays and their vulgar manifestations like packages to Lloret, oldies dancing with their Zimmers in Benidorm, and youngsters manoeuvering for dates in discos. But these are the places where chance (or God) has called me and where I have exercised my unofficial ministry.

A last-minute holiday booking landed me and a friend in the heart of disco territory, the only oldies there. No one knew what to do with us, so they appeased us with free disco tickets.

I sat in the throbbing darkness, sipping a Cola, wondering whether I would ever hear again. Word must have got round about the presence of a tame cleric, because a dribble of clients approached my table seeking the consolations of religion.

I persuaded one girl who had been stood up to

pray for courage and try again, trusting God a little more and boys considerably less. And another to face the fact that the film star who was only working incognito as a waiter while he was 'resting' probably wouldn't be waiting for her when she returned next year. And the panicky teenager that his pimples weren't the Marks of the Beast, but only adolescence.

No chaplains, as far as I could see, looked after these youngsters. And there are millions of them suffering from love, sunburn, sex and commercial hype.

Dietrich Bonhoeffer warned about the gap that was growing between the life of the boulevard and the religious ghetto. You can see the chasm widening on every Costa. In the local churches, a few old ladies in black shawls mumble their rosaries. In the bars, defiant, blue-rinsed lovelies seek company with quiet desperation. The two never meet. The permanent foreign chaplains minister to the permanent foreign residents, but are not geared to cope with transient hordes. No religious presence I know helps with the despair in departure lounges on a hot summer during another vindictive industrial dispute.

My teacher and I are separated not just by years but by new patterns of life and experience. People's needs have changed; so have their choices and the spirituality they must apply to them.

Also people live longer and stay younger. In their Third Age, provided their bodies don't let them down, they won't sleep by the fire, shrouded in shawls, reciting pieties as insurance. They'll be whizzing round Britain on Awayday tickets or sitting astride a stool beside a bar in Benidorm.

My teacher taught me to tell people how to be good. But in a hedonistic time, people are more interested in how to be happy. I believe that both, tackled honestly, lead back to the same source, God, so there's no point in being a spiritual snob. Happiness, it's true, has not been a religious favourite. Spiritual high-flyers in the past have usually been powered by poverty, frustration and depression. 'Blessed be misery' has been the name of the religious game. But happiness, holidays and satisfaction can also make people good and generous, though the metaphysics of happiness haven't yet been recognised, and only adverts and commercials fill the gap – which is dangerous because they connect outward objects and inner states too directly.

Perhaps some Sisters, Brothers or Fathers who've given up working in schools and nursing homes for the privileged will find a new vocation among the migrant packaged masses seeking vulgar happiness under commercial guidance. There are millions of them, and there will be even more in the new Europe, if it works.

Soft Religion

My mother's naturally happy, but I can be a miserable so-and-so because I'm a worrier. Which is why I was attracted to religion, because its teachings can be pretty miserable too.

So I'm not really the right person to wish everyone Happy New Year or Happy Easter or Happy Passover as easily and enthusiastically as I do, because some people ask me how you get one. My mother might know, but she smiles to herself and won't say, so I'll try to answer from my own experience.

You can certainly be happy for a while if you leave out life's nasty bits – which is why I went on a package holiday and read no newspapers, only Regency romances which never mentioned Regency smells or the horrors of the slave trade. I enjoyed holiday religion too, which was commercial but kind. Messages of love were everywhere and a record repeated again and again that we'd all live for evermore. It certainly worked. I became happy and rather nice, and old ladies loved me.

But happiness that comes easy like that doesn't last. When you get home, you need real religion to cope with real life and its real problems, such as taxes, disease and toothache. Soft religion isn't strong enough, and it's odd but only the difficult religious doctrines give you the support you need.

A Christian friend told me how original sin helps

him. 'It means,' he said 'I'm an imperfect person in an imperfect world, who can never get it right. So I do my best, give it to God and don't worry.'

And I personally rely a lot on the Last Judgment – once again a difficult doctrine, but a comfort if you're in the public eye, because then you're the focus of a lot of criticism, which isn't easy to cope with. Some of it is projection, of course, but some of it's true, so you can't just dismiss it. But if you concentrate on God's judgment, you don't get so battered by other people's, and you get the strength to be objective.

As you've gathered, I'm suspicious of happiness that comes from changing your surroundings but not yourself, and of all soft religion. If, on spiritual journeys, you have to choose between a hard way and a soft way, choose the hard; if you can endure it, it is the more reliable.

The Oil in the Machine

Spring is breaking out all over, when a young man's fancy turns to love. Birds do it, bees do it, and some do it once too often. Even I am invited to give lectures on sex and spirituality, though approaching my old-age pension. But though the sap is rising in me too, I hesitate, remembering an awkward question of my mother's before she went into a home.

We'd been watching a wildlife film, in which sex was nature's bait for reproduction, and in it a female fish annexes her partner, turning him into a pimple on her own body. 'What was God thinking of when He created sex?' exclaimed my mother. 'It could have been organised better.'

I won't comment, theologically it's too tricky, but it's even more puzzling now that evolution's taken another turn in us higher animals, separating sex from reproduction, so that some sublimate it into religion or hit the bottle, while others use it to dominate, give pleasure, or just to fall asleep.

'Didn't they teach you the answer at your seminary?' complains my mother.

Seminaries are better at love and marriage, I tell her; agony aunts are more matter of fact. In any case, religion's never given me The Answer – just enough bits of truth to live by. Having learnt them the hard way, I'm not going to waste them on my own mother in her sunset years.

Actually I did learn some very tough and true bits

in my seminary – that what feels instinctively isn't necessarily right, and that the sex instinct is so immediate that children, the weak and the disadvantaged need protection, for like all God's gifts, it must be used to help, not harm others. Also that promises made in the heat of passion should be kept if possible, even the trivial ones.

Later on, from my pastoral work, I realised that sexually fulfilled people are, generally speaking, nicer to others. Like the oil in a machine, sex prevents friction. And we should respect the physical needs of people in institutions, such as the disabled, the long-term sick and prisoners.

But I learnt one of the most important spiritual lessons, listening to people's stories in the secular discos of the permissive Sixties: that though sex was fun as well as a theological problem, it's still not the purpose of our life on earth and if you make it so, you'll make yourself trivial.

Who Are You?

Jews like jokes about changing names.

On a luxury liner, a lady welcomes a newcomer to the bridge table. 'I'm Mrs Colquhoun,' she says. 'And this is Mrs McCorquodale and this is Mrs Canterbury.'

'How extraordinary!' exclaims the newcomer knowingly. 'My name's Cohen too!'

I'm still sensitive about the subject, because in 1944 my form master read out a letter from my mother, requesting that I no longer be addressed as Lionel Bluestein but as Lionel Blue. Amid the catcalls, I muttered maledictions on both my parents. White, Green and Brown were fine, but Blue was odd, and suggestive of blue stories and blue jokes. They'd botched it again.

I wasn't surprised. I'd already borne a Yiddish and a Hebrew name as well as the one on my birth certificate, each with different expectations to go with it. But going against adults was a mug's game, so I ironed out my accent, studied for Oxford and became an almost English gentleman, to match my new name. If my grandparents had landed in Leith, not London, I'd now be MacBlue, trying to throw a hammer in tartan trousers.

One of the main reasons I went into religion at Oxford was to rediscover the real me behind those names. I was attracted by the text: 'I have called you by your name, you are Mine'. But perhaps I overdid the religion because I became a rabbi and landed in more role-playing, for clerics, like politicians and other public figures, have to fulfil the fantasies of their followers. I had to look benign when babies wee-ed on me while I blessed them. But fortunately (or so it seemed to me then), not being married, I was spared playing holy happy families – which was silly because making up after rows can be the important bit, or so I'm told.

And that is why my real religious moment doesn't come during the public Jewish New Year services, for instance, but afterwards when, divested of robes and role-playing, I sit alone in an empty synagogue, seeking my true identity, and how God knows me.

I recommend such meditation, even if you've got a normal name like Smith or MacTavish and your New Year begins on the first of January, not the middle of September.

Because if you don't find your true self, you end up identifying yourself with your property or, if you work in the media like me, with your publicity. And when both drop away – as they assuredly will – meaning will drop out of your life. Or even worse, you'll acquire an identity from your fantasies or your possessions, or worse, a groupie identity by joining a mob.

Looking around a kilt shop in Glasgow, I discovered I wasn't free from a bit of falsity myself. Apparently there's a Blue sub-clan somewhere in the Western Isles and I'm minded to wear a wee bit of their tartan myself. But after this, do I dare?

Love

An old Oxford friend complained, 'Like all clergy-men on sex, you raise questions you don't answer.'

Well, some I can't! I can't, for example, say what God was thinking of when he created it. But I can add this personal footnote on sex and spirituality which came together for me when we were both at Oxford over forty years ago.

It's hard to recall how innocent and ignorant we were. I was nearly twenty but still uncertain of a woman's anatomy. My little knowledge came from law reports and *Forever Amber*. And I wasn't alone. In those pre-Pill days, fear discouraged any pre-marital research. An illegitimate baby ruined a girl's life, two women together were ostracised and two men went to jail.

By chance I bumped into religion just when my passions were about to explode, and soared like a sex-propelled rocket through ritual to mystical chats with a divine lover. It was only a substitute, but it stopped me becoming a very nasty person and would sort itself out when I got the real thing.

I got it some years later, but to my surprise my see-through presence didn't fade. In fact, I often preferred its inner voice in places of worship to human beings at parties. Physical desires come and go, weakening with age, but that substitute love has remained, underpinning my life.

There are times when circumstance or conscience

119

say no to sex for all of us. If you can find God in your frustration, He can help you go ahead of your body into bliss. Don't be bullied by sexual fashion. Sublimation isn't a dirty word. It can also be an opportunity. In the frustration years, it was my way to real love, and it might be the same for you.

Self-Deception

I've received another letter enquiring if I know a chap who says he's a rabbi and also my assistant, and who needs help because his car's broken down. I'm afraid I don't recognise the rabbi. I've no assistant and my friends don't use my name in that way.

I sympathise with the writer because I've also wondered whether to trust or not to trust. We'd all like to be as generous and innocent as doves, but the world's a tricky place, so we're also advised to be as subtle as serpents – and the two don't combine easily.

Some of the world's tricks, of course, are not of human making. My elderly great-aunt, for example, visited her flatmate in hospital and, startled by the hoist and feeding-cup, exclaimed strangely, 'So that's the blinking end of it!'

I know what she meant. Old age is a bizarre trick life plays on all of us, and you have to be a Rembrandt to see the soul shining through the decaying flesh to make sense of it.

But some of the world's tricks are definitely of human making. For example, have you noticed how aggressors no longer kill their enemies; they just 'cleanse' them? The propaganda tricks of Hitler and Stalin turned 'nice' people, no different from us, into murderers.

But just identifying the tricks of the world and of

other people is a kind of avoidance. We also have to identify our own. Even our religion can become tricky if we use it to avoid growing up or taking responsibility for our own decisions. Long prayers can be used to stop God getting a word in edge-ways, and ritual to dress up our fantasies. And then there are the small ways we cheat ourselves. I deceive myself, for example, every time I diet. When I go on an ordinary package holiday, I pretend I'm used to casinos, nightclubs and high living.

Such tricks may seem small, but they can be serious and even fatal. There's a hidden warning in this little joke if you've got ears to hear it. A pretentious couple go on a posh yachting holiday. The husband, who pretends he can swim, has to be rescued and lies on the beach gasping. A lifeguard rushes towards him, shouting 'Out of the way! He needs artificial respiration.' But his wife bars the way, insisting, 'Only real respiration or nothing!'

To help the world become a less tricky place, we have to start with ourselves. Here's a helpful tip I learnt at retreats for alcoholics. Some begin with a 'feelings session' at which they come clean to God, each other and themselves about their own self-deceptions – not to judge or blame, but to face them.

And so at the beginning of the week, on a park bench or in a place of worship, I've got into the habit of examining my own self-deceptions. It's a trick worth knowing, which makes me less of a nuisance to myself and to others. I recommend it.

And Where to Find It

It's been one of those weeks. At the beginning, I double-dated myself and two guests arrived for dinner just as I was going out with someone else. And at the end of the week, an old friend rang as I was pausing for thought and, distracted, I enquired how he was and how was his dear grandmother. 'You should know,' he said sweetly, 'since you buried her.' What does one say?

To calm myself, I harvested a crop of travel brochures to daydream about future holidays with happy endings.

But realism breaks in. I remember holidays which didn't turn out that happy and, being honest, the problem wasn't in the brochures but in me. Which is why I recommend ten minutes' meditation in the departure lounge before they call your flight. (Yes, there is a chapel, but where? And can you break in?) I know a packed departure lounge isn't purpose-built for meditation, but try, because what really makes you happy might not be what you think, and a little reflection can save you a lot of misery.

The happiest holiday I ever had was one of my earliest, and the least promising. Our hotel hadn't even been built, and the furniture was fixed firmly to the floor, so we couldn't walk off with it. Our party huddled together after breakfast in the only café open. In dripping macs and raincoats, we sat on a line of bar stools like a forlorn Sunday-school outing, gulping down glasses of passion fruit, aniseed and banana liqueurs to keep warm.

'It's like the Blitz,' someone remarked reflectively and, spontaneously, we burst into 'Bless 'em All' and 'Run, Rabbit, Run' and 'Rule Britannia', alarming the locals by our strange bellicosity. We couldn't stop laughing. I remember that freezing holiday with warm feelings. We were so supportive to each other, it was like the war!

That holiday taught me that happiness isn't in fitments and fixtures, it's in you. Things make you comfortable, but only giving happiness to others makes you happy. It's the mean who are miserable. They're so busy calculating whether they got the better holiday deal, they've no time to enjoy it.

Insecurity

My accountant is calling this afternoon to explain the Budget and put my papers in order, if he can find them among my recipes, theological notes and bits of chocolate. He's a kind and forgiving chap and I hope God will be the same at my Last Judgment. But I still feel twitchy and embarrassed because I buy silly luxuries I don't need to bolster my ego. Like many people, I cover my insecurity with consumerism.

I knew a nice peasant family once, who force-fed me on pasta in their cosy cottage by the Med when I was ill. Then they invited me to their new home. Inside two massive doors, a marble staircase curved to the first floor, where the family received me po-faced under a plastic chandelier. They offered no pasta and I felt rejected. Later, I learnt they couldn't because their new home had no kitchen, the doors were dummies and the family inhabited the stair-well. Because of insecurity, they had sacrificed their hospitality for show.

My grandmother, also a peasant woman, suffered from the same sense of inferiority after she caught the English class bug. She saved her pennies for a parlour. It was the only room in the house that got daylight, but that was excluded by crimson plush curtains. On a horsehair sofa, by a teak table with dry, dead flowers and a black marble clock which didn't work, my grandmother

125

also 'received' for two hours every Sabbath, trying to look snooty like the middle-class ladies. That parlour gave me the willies and they couldn't coax me into it.

My mother's insecurity grew even more acute watching Hollywood high life on the screens of her local Roxy, Troxy and Odeon. So in the Depression, she bought a chrome cocktail cabinet on the never-never which lit up and played 'Roll Out the Barrel'. My mother stood behind it, casually inviting her neighbours to a highball. They compromised on tea, prudently, because the cabinet only contained sticky Passover wine, for my father detested drink and my mother disliked the taste. Even as a child, such play-acting embarrassed me.

But what about my own insecurity? To be honest, I became a rabbi from mixed motives, some right, some wrong. Among the wrong ones was my need for status. I wore elaborate and uncomfortable robes to convince myself and God I was special, because I didn't believe it.

If you too suffer from the same self-doubt, here's a more direct way to deal with it than a spending spree, and it won't cost an arm or a leg. Just say these words to yourself each morning till their message sinks in:

'I am a unique creation, a one-off. God never made anyone exactly like me before and never will again – in His eyes I am very special. Both my good and bad points play their part in His plan. I will have opportunities today which will never re-occur and they are meant for me only and no other.'

When my accountant calls at five o'clock this afternoon, I'll mumble these words under my breath. Why not join in?

Fantasy and Fancies

It's the last day of term and my class takes time off from theology to munch egg mayonnaise and trade tips on holidays.

One student recommends reading a Bible in the language of the country you're going to. You won't need a dictionary for the popular bits like the Ten Commandments and the Twenty-third Psalm, and it will give tone to your conversation at the hotel bar.

My own advice is meaner. Before you go, look for last year's souvenirs in charity shops. They go dirt-cheap and you won't have to lug back badly wrapped bird cages across Europe.

We say goodbye emotionally – for some it will be for the last time, and as their chatter dies away, I sit in the empty college chapel, waiting for whatever comes to mind.

What comes is a curious holiday phantasy. Our plane touches down at a Mediterranean airport, and while the rest of the holidaymakers wait for their coach in the sizzling sun, a private hotel car draws up and a driver in a peaked cap deferentially opens the door for me. I nod to my fellow travellers, deprecating my superiority, but kindly invite some to a drink in my special-supplement hotel.

Now if this makes you queasy, it makes me want to vomit, and I'm tempted to retreat to some safe prayer for piety or sweetness or such. Instead I ask

God for the guts to go on with my fantasy – whatever the embarrassment.

What follows is even worse. In reverie I graciously receive my guests in my hotel, and carelessly command the waiter to bring us brandy – 'six star at least,' I say *sotto voce*. 'Golly, you don't get booze like that in our pub,' chortle my guests. The waiter raises an eyebrow, and we commiserate silently.

'Yuk,' I say to God, 'I never believed I could be so cheap.' But He is merciful, and another picture comes to mind, of a poor East End boy patronised by kind rich relations and friends. It's me, and fifty-five years on, I'm still compensating!

But I'm comforted because most people have some silly phantasy tucked away in their minds. Some are snobbish, like mine; some sadistic, with jackboots; some pathetic; some funny and some curious. We can't help having them – they're the scars of wounds life inflicted on us long ago. But we can stop making our fantasies real by deciding not to act them out in life, for that's when they turn dangerous, even spilling into politics. And that's why I no longer ask for far-fetched or silly things in prayer – just the courage to see myself as I am, and the humility to accept what I see.

To set the record straight, for my real holiday I've booked a cheap and cheerful bargain package. You don't get six-star brandy, of course, but a few years ago we got a really hot cup of tea and three free biscuits, which was *lovely*.

Feeding the Soul

Like many of you, I'm looking forward to my
holiday. Life's been hectic – and I want it to be a
happy holiday, so that this time we'll all come back
speaking to each other.

But a friend told me you're only happy when
your body, mind and soul are in harmony. He
didn't tell me how to get such harmony, so I
invented this game for myself. In my imagination, I
invite my body, mind and soul to tea, as it were, and
while I pretend to pour out and pass see-through
scones, they tell each other their needs. It sounds
silly but it's the only way I bring the different bits of
me together. I try it again, and my body and mind
say they're happy with my holiday because there's a
buffet, two swimming pools, and ruins that my
mind can brood over. Only my soul is silent – once
again I haven't listened to its needs. I've been so
busy with religion that I've mislaid my soul, I tell
myself facetiously – perhaps I've lost it.

I sit back startled, for these words aren't funny
but deadly serious – since all relationships die
unless you give them time and attention. Would it
matter if my soul died of neglect, if I lost it?

Well, it's my soul that turns my failures into
compassion. It's my soul that shows me heaven in
unlikely places and people – and I couldn't do my
hospital work without it. It helps me love people I
don't like and put up with people I can't stand, who

snore or who've got BO or both. And as it's the only bit of me that can survive death, I'd better cultivate it before it's too late because I'm sixty-three! Also, if it went, I'd be terrified of the emptiness it would leave in the centre of myself, which would fill up with silly pretentious selves and false values that die with the world and have no share in eternal life.

I shiver because this is sad stuff and try to restore my spirits with some jolly Jewish holiday jokes – but they're not just jolly, they're also warnings against the vanities that try to replace my soul.

Like the story of the couple who go to Rome and when they return boast about the celebrities they dined with. 'But did you dine with the Pope?' someone asks.

'Sure,' said the wife, 'who else?'

'And how did you find him?'

The wife puckered her brow. 'Him I liked,' she said, 'her I didn't take to.'

Jewish jokes like that are funny but also frightening, because without my soul I could become a name-dropper too. So reluctantly, though I've got piles of work, I ring up a retreat centre and book in for two days' silence before I go off on holiday. My friend was right – unless I listen to my soul, my happy holiday's had it. And yours, too, if you think it through.

LOVE THY NEIGHBOUR
(AS THYSELF)

Happy Families

My mother and aunt eventually needed more care than I could provide for them in the house we shared in Finchley.

It's time, I said, to talk about sheltered accommodation and homes with medical back-up. My mother muttered in Yiddish to make me feel guilty, and I retaliated, exhibiting the stress spots on my arm. The real problem was my mother's reluctance to recognise old age. She still sees herself as a business lady toting a typewriter or queening it in a café, like Marlene Dietrich, with the boys in the back room. But she has a weak spot. She feels guilty too because she's not a Yiddishe momme who sacrifices her all to her baby – which is me, and occasionally I play on it.

I may hold the stronger cards, but men are the weaker sex. My weak points, and my mother's sussed them out, are my past sermons on family life and my religious role-playing. She's not averse to using them and playing the guilt game on me.

'Lionel,' she said to me in an Indian restaurant, 'don't have any children, dear. They can cause you so much suffering! Believe me, I know.' Now I'm her only child, and I watched her narrowly as she knocked back another vindaloo.

The truth is that our feelings towards those we love aren't simple, but complex. Alongside the love, there's a hidden agenda of manipulation and unspoken criticism. If you deny them, they don't disappear; they just do more damage.

So I wandered into a place of worship, invoked the spirit of truth and faced up to what I really felt about my nearest and dearest – which of course includes God.

This last is the most difficult, but necessary, because the same games we play with our earthly mothers and fathers, we also play with our Father in Heaven, and this invalidates a lot of our religion if we don't acknowledge it. But since God, unlike us, really is pure love and truth, as we say so often in our prayers, then with Him at least we can afford to risk it and come clean.

Making Peace with Your Parents

Another Jewish new year; another visit to the cemetery to say the traditional prayers and put another pebble on my father's grave, as Abraham did on Sarah's four thousand years ago. Near the grave, I bump into a depressed colleague coming from a funeral. I commiserate, because death releases a lot of guilt and anger in the mourners, which they unload on the minister. I know, because I did it myself when my father died.

My poor pa lived in a matriarchal society, like many Jewish men of his generation. They were providers for their mothers, wives and children; they recited the ritual prayers but never decided policy. They reigned, but did not rule. I remembered my father's friend in the pre-World War days, a pious little man who'd tried to stop his women-folk quarrelling. They tenderly removed him, telling him to return to his prayers. Many hours later, my father heard a moan coming from the airing cupboard, where he found his friend marooned on the top shelf. In the heat of battle, they had forgotten where they'd put him. Such petticoat rule must have been galling to my father, who was a macho boxer. As I stand at his grave, I remember how his submission had so irritated me, and I also remember his self-sacrifice, which I never appreciated.

I want to say sorry but in one sense it's too late, because he was buried long ago. Yet in another

sense it's not, because our dead parents still live in
us, shaping our attitudes even if we're not aware of
it.

Which is why in prayer, I still find it easier to
think of God as my friend, or as the brother I never
had, rather than as a patriarchal father figure. And
because my father was such a fine athlete, I opted
out and became clumsy, because I couldn't com-
pete.

I did once suggest you invite your body, mind and
soul to an imaginary tea party. And there, with the
help of the Holy Spirit, listen to what they had to
say to you and to each other about their frustrations
and needs. If this device helped you make peace
with yourself, then do the same with your dead
parents who continue to live inside you as part of
you. In your imagination, let them tell you their side
of the story and you tell them what you didn't dare
to when they were alive. A cemetery or silent chapel
is good for such plain speaking because it can be
quite painful, and you may need a place where God
feels close. But that's how you get rid of your guilt
and anger, and begin to live in charity with yourself
and others.

During my summer holiday, I took time off to
watch TV newsreels, gripped by the battles in
Bosnia and the Middle East. They seemed such a
male affair. The ferocious fighters and competing
politicians were all men, while the women just
suffered and watched. And when the soldiers were
interviewed, they talked about their duty to their
fatherlands and their gallant ancestors. How much

better if those young men had used their courage to understand their fathers, rather than repeating their fathers' mistakes on battlefields and proving their own manhood with murder. After all, you don't have to be Jewish to be honest with yourself in a cemetery.

Criminal Education

After I blacked out in Bruges and then fell into a supermarket freezer, they took away my driving licence. But there were unexpected compensations and on crowded trains I now peer over my fellow traveller's shoulder for a free read of his tabloid.

It's riveting stuff. A minister is chasing a choirboy and a matron is chasing the minister. A girl has caught her fiancé canoodling with her grandma. What should she feel? 'Grateful it wasn't her grandpa', growls the paper's owner and then adds defensively, 'It's educational – learning from the fall of other people, like.'

I agree hypocritically because I want to share his paper and try to ingratiate myself by telling him about the teacher who complained to Mrs Cohen that her son was disruptive.

'Be firm,' she said, 'I'm no besotted mother. Whenever he's naughty, slap the kid sitting next to him.'

'But why?' said the bewildered teacher.

'Oh, my boy's bright,' she said, 'he'll get the message.'

My companion is silent; he does not see the joke and turns the page. We read on, this time about a mother who's battered her baby. 'They should give her life,' he says.

This time, it's my turn to be silent. I remember the day I bought a puppy. I patted it, provided it with food, water and a rubber bone, and tottered to bed. I'd been up all night with a dying woman and I was walloped. Every time I got to sleep, the puppy howled, and finally in a frenzy of exhaustion I slapped it hard several times. I went to sleep while it whimpered and have never forgiven myself.

I get out at Marble Arch feeling like a criminal, and remember that Marble Arch was once called Tyburn, where they hanged criminals who'd first been drawn and quartered. At a fast-food counter nearby, I do some comfort eating and remember a poem by a criminal in the Middle Ages, who before his trial imagined himself swinging from such a gibbet. 'Brothers,' says his skeleton to the passers-by, 'if you take pity on these bones, perhaps God will take pity on you. Human beings aren't always responsible for their actions, so pray to God to forgive us all.' I do just that and press five pounds on an astonished charity collector to confirm my prayer.

Returning on the Underground that evening, again I can't resist reading my neighbour's paper. Something in us is excited by the misfortunes of others and it's best to admit it. Those stories can be educational, I tell myself, provided you do two things. After you've read one, say to yourself, 'There but for the grace of God go I.' And when you turn the page, 'May God forgive us all together.'

Life's Travellers

Bruised and battered in a Spanish airport, I grab my luggage – just in time, because as we're let out, a planeload of holidaymakers from Hamburg swarms in. And their advance guard battles with our stragglers for *lebensraum*.

One new arrival accosts me angrily, demanding his baggage in bad Spanish; because I am dark and scruffy, he mistakes me for a local. I reply sharply in pidgin German. 'Entschuldigen, – sorry, mate, but I'm a traveller too!'

Later on, recovering in a bar, I remember these words; I'd spoken wiser than I knew. Because we're all travellers; life's like a journey and this world is an airport, not our final destination.

This isn't original. The ancient Hebrews had a similar idea because their forty years wandering through the wilderness was burnt into their memory.

Sometimes when I wake up in the morning, I remember their experience. Because like them I'm also frightened of ogres and giants I might meet. Chapter Sixteen of the Book of Exodus helps me because it's not just pious, but practical. It describes how the children of Israel only gathered enough manna for one day's journey, not storing any for the next, except before the Sabbath when they were allowed a double share.

Applying this to my own situation, I leave

tomorrow to God and concentrate on today which is manageable. I don't waste time on future fears but ask for courage not to dive back under my duvet. Then I concentrate on my modern manna, my cornflakes and my morning cuppa. It's my double portion of manna to remember the sweetness stored up for the righteous at journey's end.

Queen and Country

An old-time Jewish couple are given a Continental holiday. Marvelling, they make their way to the beach, he in his black gabardine and she in her shawl, astonished by the bronzed breasts and buttocks around them. Timidly she cries, 'Abie, they're laughing at us?'

'There, there, bubele,' he replies reassuringly, 'maybe they've never seen real Britishers like us before.'

My grandparents were like that.

They kept their British passport with their Bible, because Britain was the only country which had ever been decent to them. And the contents of every tin and packet had to be not just kosher but Empire produce.

'English', 'Welsh' or 'Scots' were subtleties they couldn't comprehend, but since they all spoke English, did it matter?

Well, it matters now, because the same forces which worked so violently in Yugoslavia work among us too, though in a politer British fashion. Study the backs of cars; GB isn't enough. Some add the cross of St George, and others CYM and Ecosse. A Scots driver asserted fiercely that the Queen might be Elizabeth the Second south of the border, but above it she was only the First.

Being British is important because it's the only word which unites us all, aboriginals and newcomers.

Nice people advise mutual understanding, so that we learn to like each other. I agree, but it isn't nearly enough – knowing needn't mean liking. We're so diverse, it could mean loathing. Which means we have to love each other a little – there's no other way.

Good places to experience the extra force we need, which some call God, are the holy islands off our coasts – Lindisfarne, Iona and Bardsey. Pilgrimages there make religious sense even if you're not Christian, because that's where Britain was spiritually born.

LIFE AND DEATH AND LIFE

A Sixtieth Part of Death

Here's a tip on leisurely getting up on the Sabbath, Jewish-style. It's a thank-you for all I've learnt from getting up Christian-style.

During the war, my evangelical foster-parents taught me to kneel beside my bed and present God with a list of benefits and beneficiaries. I'm grateful because it started that inner conversation which has been my life's companion.

I'm also grateful for unfussy Anglican matins, and the pure silence of a Quaker family before breakfast. Also for a dawn Catholic mass in the cockpit of a small boat in mid-North Sea, with me as the only congregation.

My earliest Jewish memory is trotting behind my father to a congregation of tailors who met for religious study and lemon tea before they clocked in at their steamy sweat shops. I felt new, and so did the world as my father and I wandered home, hand in hand, while the first light filtered through the sooty streets.

This combination of study and food ranks with prayer among Jews. So if you're not up to formal morning prayers, curl up with a Danish pastry and a religious book instead. And if you need support, some synagogues run study breakfasts, providing books and beigels — and some house-churches do the same with Bibles and croissants. Most are welcoming, because study and food together turn strangers into a religious family.

What will you get out of your religious getting up?

First, an enormous appetite. I've never seen so many doorsteps of bread consumed as in a contemplative monastery after morning meditation.

Also you recover the sense of wonder you lost as a child. You won't say, 'Not caviar and asparagus *again* for breakfast, Ma!' but 'What, caviar and asparagus again for breakfast, mother?'

And after blessing our common Creator, the giver of light, you feel at one with other early morning risers – with animals, nuns and newspaper sellers, with the men and women who work through the night.

And this feeling of oneness will increase your charity as you listen to the day's news. For example, you won't want to gloat over former ministers when they're down, but rather remember the good they've done.

Which is very prudent, because the rabbis said that sleep is a sixtieth part of death and getting up a foretaste of our own judgment and resurrection. So if you've been generous to others, God may remember the good you've done when it's your turn to sleep and not wake up in this world.

Write Your Own Obituary!

Now that my mother's older, she speaks louder and I couldn't help hearing her on the telephone.

An elderly admirer of hers had died and his son was breaking it gently to her.

'Oh, he died on Monday,' boomed my mother in deep distress. 'And the funeral's on Friday.' She paused and then said briskly, 'Now, what's news?'

How that son's jaw must have dropped!

Later on, I explained to him that my mother wasn't being evasive. She believes that the dead are quite safe in the hands of God, because her father in heaven has the same warm, indulgent love for his children as her Yiddishe father and mother had on earth for her. So, like many Jews, she dislikes talking about death but she doesn't fear it, and has no time for hell, even after the holocaust.

I've inherited her matter-of-factness. A lady complimented me on my pastry. 'You can't beat marble for rolling it out,' I cried enthusiastically. 'Cadge a bit of tombstone from the stonemason.' Well, she had another cuppa but no more cake.

Death is the one certainty for us all, so it's prudent to get acquainted. Why not sign up for a contemplative retreat and try to die to the world? Most retreats have decent beds now and even central heating. Or you could help out in a hospice. The sadness there is mixed with too much love and laughter for tragedy.

151

I'm not trying to glamorise death. I dislike pain, and all functions of the body are messy, whether it's birth, death, making love or masticating food. But a foretaste of your own mortality brings a lot of benefits. It makes you appreciate the present, and it helps you work out what's worthwhile and what's silly in your life.

Last week, for example, I had to demonstrate some live TV cooking, than which nothing is more fraught – because while you fry and chop, you also smile and chat. Before I even got to the studio, I was in a foul temper. At the hotel I couldn't find my clean shirt. Breakfast arrived just as I'd soaped myself in the shower and, caught on the hop, I'd dropped my toothpaste in the toilet. When I got to the studio, I lost my cookbook and promptly wished I were dead.

Suddenly I saw my shirt and lost toothpaste in the light of eternity and I rolled about with laughter. I even hugged a passing producer, who took it rather well, considering.

If you too lose your sense of proportion, and what with one thing and another I don't blame you, here's a spiritual exercise to get it back. *Write your own obituary*. No, I'm not kinky, and I don't think I'm suffering from any dreadful disease. I just want to tell you that death is also a gift of God which can teach you a lot about life.

Problems

When I was off the air after an epileptic blackout, two people actually gathered material for my obituary, but when I came to in hospital, I wasn't thinking of eternal life, just about the problems of this one.

I remembered a story a student told me. A man wanders the world asking, 'What is life?' Finally he hears of a sage high up on a holy mountain, and he clambers over glaciers, into the sage's presence.

'You disturb my silence,' says the sage. 'Ask three questions and go!'

'What is life?' shouts the seeker through the howling wind.

'Problems and suffering,' moaned the sage.

'And beyond those?'

'More problems, more suffering. Your third question, please.'

'Is there another mystic higher up?' hissed the seeker.

But the sage was right, and second opinions don't help. As a child I used to think that after exams, life would be problem-free – just as people think that after the recession, life will be lovely. But when we solve one problem, another takes its place. Life *IS* problems, as the sage said.

So while I waited for the doctor to stitch up my scalp, it seemed only prudent to make friends with

my problems. They might even have a message for
me.

So if you've got problems – and who hasn't –
don't curse them; make friends with them instead.
Perhaps they're trying to tell you something really
important.

Crunch Time

In my youth, studying history got me addicted to saints. Their lives were much more thrilling than film stars'. There was the one who beseeched God to help him because he was too good-looking and so God fitted him with a dog's head. Regretfully that wasn't my problem. The cry of little Thérèse of Lisieux was more relevant: 'Only the truth!'

Perhaps I was saint-starved, for 'saint' or 'holy' in Hebrew is reserved for God, not humans. Even Moses doesn't rate it.

So when a friend rang me from Rome with the latest gossip on canonisations, I was all ears. There was talk about Pope John XXIII and Pius XII, alone or in tandem; the Austrian, Franz Jagerstätter; Isabella of Spain; our own Cardinal Newman and assorted nuns.

'Do they have enough miracles?' I asked greedily because the bizarre is fascinating.

'Miracles are no longer necessary,' he sighed. I clucked sympathetically over such modernism, but had to say goodbye, because it wasn't my problem. And one of my own was sitting on the doorstep: a big black dog without a collar, abandoned in a nearby car park.

How could I let him in? I can't keep a dog I told myself; I'm away too much. A dog pound wouldn't do either, for who'd have him? Like me, he was too old. I decided to leave him some food well away

155

from the house. But that's when my saint came marching in. You were wondering about that, weren't you?

While I stared at Bonzo, and Bonzo stared at Muggins here, I remembered the Franz Jagerstätter my friend mentioned on the phone – the unpolitical Austrian worker who wouldn't fight for Hitler because he felt it wasn't right. He got sent to a non-combatant corps. But that didn't feel right either, and though his priest pleaded with him, and his bishop, and his wife, they finally beheaded him. Like Luther, he could do no other.

And I could do no other, either. You can't turn out a fellow creature into a night that's not fit for a dog. You can only calculate with your conscience so far and then the crunch comes, whether it's Hitler or a dog on your doorstep.

I don't think religious people like me have any special aptitude for politics. We're amateurs in a professional game. But we can help others recognise that crunch point, because God is in it. It's the bottom line below which you begin to lose your soul. People like Wilberforce knew it when he worked against slavery. An SS officer I once met, knew it when he gave water to thirsty Jewish babies. Franz Jagerstätter knew it and so should you. It will decide your fate, not just in this world but in whatever worlds you will inhabit beyond it.

But to return to the dog. Well, he slept soundly that night on a blanket by the living-room radiator. And I lay awake listening to his snores and worrying what I'd do with him the next morning. I finally fell asleep, deciding only to call him Jake, short for Jagerstätter, because that's whom he owed his warm bed to.

It might be no miracle, but God willing, taking in Jake might help Franz Jagerstätter's cause in Rome. We all need reminding that not everything in life is negotiable.

Seeing the World as God Sees It

Before I went on holiday, I booked in for two days' quiet in a friary – which means monks, not fish. No, I'm not convert material and I'm not going to fall into a font. I go there because they're contemplatives who understand why I need to put a foot in heaven and from there, see the world again as God sees it.

I've seen it that way twice before, and it's the basis of all I've ever been trying to say. The first time was after God came alive to me in a Quaker meeting. For two months, people's faces became windows through which I glimpsed heaven. The second time was shorter. Human love had gone wrong. I felt desperate, and then the world began to glow again with divine love.

But you don't have to go to a friary to get a toehold in heaven. It's all around us and the doors to it are everywhere. If, for example, you're going on holiday to Holland, sit in front of Vermeer's *View of Delft* for half an hour, because he saw that city the way God saw it. From personal experience, I can tell you that the stillness lingers on in you long after – even in a Dutch disco.

If you're on a package holiday to Majorca, look for the small letters *eremita* (hermitage) on a large-scale map. They're hidden on hilltops a few miles from the lager bars. There aren't many full-time hermits around these days, so why not become a part-time one for a few hours, and extend your holiday into a different dimension?

But heaven can also just happen. One case occurred in a hot airport departure lounge during an industrial dispute. The bar had run dry, and a thirsty lady drank half a plastic bottle of water from her neighbour's bag. But it wasn't ordinary water; it was holy water, blessed at a shrine. Afterwards she said, 'I felt weird with that inside me because I had to be nice to everybody afterwards.'

I know what she meant – the outward sign of that inner experience is compassion.

Some time after that Quaker meeting, I was watching a friend scribbling while he listened to the news. I was curious and reached out to read what he'd written. He'd summarised the news items something like this: eight beauty queens; one million, four hundred thousand and twenty-two unemployed; three rapes; two car crashes. And then, to my astonishment, he'd added those numbers up. Grand total: one million, four hundred thousand and thirty-five, he'd written.

'But that's total nonsense.' I laughed.

'Yes,' he said wearily, 'to us, those news items are only meaningless numbers and that's our tragedy.'

I suddenly understood what he was getting at. But after you've glimpsed the world as God sees it, news items can no longer be meaningless numbers. You feel them as flesh and blood that can laugh and cry, like you. That's the reward, as well as the price you pay for soul-searching in a friary.

Dogged Determination

I have often thought about my teachers at school, at university and at my seminary. But the one who taught me most about the really important things in life was in fact my dog – Re'ach. (*Re'ach Nicho'ach* means 'sweet odour' in the Hebrew Bible.)

I found her in a pet shop. She was all-black, part-Retriever, part-Alsatian with big feet and a suspicious nature. Perhaps she was the runt of the litter.

I don't think she was my child-substitute. She was more like the sister I never had. At the time I was not good at relationships, and my relationship with her was the only one that worked.

So she went everywhere with me, even to synagogue, where her habitual mournful expression was much admired at memorial services. She also stood up and sat down with the mourners (wondering what was in it for doggie) and this was considered cute.

What did she teach me? Well, I had been in love before, but she was the first creature I ever loved – the first one I ever took responsibility for.

For a dog, food and affection are closely linked. In Jewish life, the same is true. We ate together. She ate my fish and chips and I pinched her dog-chocolates. But she didn't want her fish on the floor. She wanted it out of a newspaper, like me, and gradually she pushed her dog-bowl closer and closer to the table, even barking for a chair, testing the barrier that separated dogs from humans, just as I was testing the barrier that separated me from heaven. She taught me a lot about being upwardly mobile.

She was also demanding, like all great teachers. The Talmud advises against doctors who don't charge – the implication being that their services will be worth no more than you paid for them.

Now all great teachers do demand. You buy a dog as you go into religion, to get something out of it. After a while you find that you've bitten off more than you've bargained for and instead of the animal or the Almighty serving your ends, you are serving theirs. Then you either give up a lot of your life, or else you give away the dog or give up religion. And with God or a dog, you can't fix the terms.

The messengers of God in human life are various. In the Bible, Balaam's ass was outstanding in perspicacity. God's messenger to me, His angel, was a humble dog (though Re'ach was never humble). 'Who is your servant but a dog?' I read on an ancient inscription in a museum. How true, I thought. If she had had a tombstone, that should have been her epitaph.

Happy Ending

While Parliament's been considering Europe's political problems, I've been considering a European spiritual one, posed by a chap who'd come back from Bombay, where he'd been sleeping on the pavement with India's poor. He'd forgotten, he said, how sad we looked here. We had so much but couldn't enjoy it. And our religion didn't help us, he added – it was so miserable.

He was right. Despite my nice home and fairly firm faith, I was pretty miserable myself. But then a friend came along to cheer me up and he carried me off to the Continent to an exhibition of European art.

'I don't want tortured saints and droopy virgins,' I grumbled, as he led me to the Early Romanesque galleries. But there, my spirits began to lift. The colours were as bright as boiled sweets. The Hebrew prophets were nice old codgers I'd like to have shared my wine with; Jesus was a trusty shepherd and his mother a comfy, country woman.

But in the Gothic galleries, my museum gloom returned. The prophets looked meaner and leaner; the holy family didn't seem a particularly happy one, and there was a lot more blood about. Why did they make religion so unhappy, I wondered? But then, why do we make ourselves so unhappy, when, as the chap said, we've been given so much?

My friend orders coffee, and tells me to buck up

163

and get on with my holiday postcards. Obediently I begin one to my therapist. 'I'm having a very happy holiday,' I write, and then pause, adding 'But WHY?' in block letters.

Actually I know why we Europeans aren't happy. It's because something's gone sour in our religion and we've turned the God of love into a sadist. Some are frightened of happiness because they think they're tempting Providence. Some misuse religion to punish themselves. Because they can't forgive themselves, they don't believe God can either. Some believe God actually enjoys our misery. My friend, who's a minister like me and a Scot, tells me of a church leader who cries from the fires of hell, 'Lord, I didna ken! I didna ken!' And God tartly replies, 'Y'ken the noo.'

But that's no giggle because it's devil worship, not God worship. True religion means believing that the God who created us, loves us and cares for us, and has prepared a happy ending for us despite all the evidence to the contrary.

My friend says I should affirm my belief in that happy ending by ordering myself a treat. I do, and become much nicer to everybody after munching marzipan.

Why don't you treat yourself too today, not as an indulgence, of course, but as a theological statement to show you also believe in a good God who wants you to enjoy the world He created without hurting others. So I wish you a happy day and I'm sure God does too, so it's over to you!